It Works for Me with High-Impact Practices

Shared Tips for Effective Teaching

By Charlie Sweet, Hal Blythe, & Russell Carpenter

NEW FORUMS PRESS INC.

Published in the United States of America
by New Forums Press, Inc.1018 S. Lewis St.
Stillwater, OK 74074
www.newforums.com

Copyright © 2018 by New Forums Press, Inc.

All rights reserved. No part of this publication may be reproduced or transmitted in any form or by any means, electronic or mechanical, including photocopy, or any information storage or retrieval system, without permission in writing from the publisher.

Library of Congress Cataloging-in-Publication Data Pending

This book may be ordered in bulk quantities at discount from New Forums Press, Inc., P.O. Box 876, Stillwater, OK 74076 [Federal I.D. No. 73 1123239]. Printed in the United States of America.

ISBN 10: 1-58107-320-8
ISBN 13: 978-1-58107-320-1

Table of Contents

Preface vii

An Introduction to High-Impact Practices ix

I. First-Year Seminars and Experiences 1
    What Factors Make First-Year Undergraduate Experiences Successful? 2
    OMG—An Orientation to Media Genres for College Freshmen 4

II. Common Intellectual Experiences 7
    Picture This 8
    Using the Deathly Hallows: Combining High-Impact Practices
        for First-Year Success 10
    Improving Course Plans Via Standardized Committee Review 13

III. Writing-Intensive Courses 15
    Developing Scientific Thinking Through Writing 16
    A Case of Their Own 18
    Getting Rid of the Research Paper 19
    Writing in the Discipline—Learning the Discourse
        of Future Professional Communities 21

IV. Collaborative Assignments and Projects 25
    How Structured Small Groups (Cooperative Learning)
        Can Motivate Students 26
    Helping Introverts Thrive During Cooperative Group Work 29
    12 Step Recovery Program for Lectureholics 32
    Learning the Agile Way with Iterative and Incremental Projects 39
    Effective and Interactive Group Assignments in an Online Course 42
    The Promise and Challenges of Synchronous Online Cooperative Learning 44
    Using Oral History for Collaborative Projects 48
    Five Approaches to Implementing End-of-Course Group Projects 51
    Creating Collaborative Learning with Storytelling 52
    Collaborative Lesson Planning: It Works For Me 54

    Weaving Collaboration Throughout a Course 57
    Pairing High School and College Students So They Can Learn
        from Each Other 60
    Student-Organized Speaker Visits: A Diversity of Voices...............................62
    Team Work Does Not Have to Be a Bad Thing..63
    Introducing Students to Tools to Support Collaboration 66

V. Undergraduate Research 69
    Scholarly and Creative Undergraduate Learning Partnership
        Team (SCULPT): Triple Areas of Focus 70
    Opening the Doors of Research Laboratories to All...73
    Involving Undergraduate Students in Research 75
    An Interview Project for the Arts Classroom 77
    A Research Laboratory Course as a High-Impact Practice 79
    Developing a Collegial Relationship with Undergraduate
        Research Students..82
    Facilitating Research Engagement and Student Success..................................84

VI. Diversity/Global Learning 89
    A New Framework for 21st Century Classrooms...90
    A Passport to Innovation: Teaching Abroad 93
    Making Immersion Experiences During Multicultural Training
        Appropriate and Meaningful for Minority Students..................................95
    What Makes a Good Study Abroad Program 98
    Hip Hip Here and Away..101
    Creating Culturally Responsive Classrooms 103
    Can 100 People Tell a Meaningful Story?..108
    Discovering the Use of Interactive Scenarios to Address
        Diversity/Global Learning...112
    Using Students' Second Language to Tackle Prejudice and Misconceptions 116

VII. Service-Learning/Community-Based Learning 119
    Making Play Not Just for Fun: Service-Learning Project
        in Children's Museum 120
    University-Level Factors Affecting Outcomes
        of Community-Based Learning 123
    Changing Lives and Minds: A Win-Win 125
    Tiered Journaling: Multiple Paths to Reflecting on Service Learning 127

Service Learning in the Visual Arts 130
Highlight Your Students' Work: Art Show (but not by artists)! 132

VIII. Internships 135
Why an Internship 136
One Size Doesn't Fit All 138
Internships with Impact: Secondary Mathematics Teacher Education 140

IX. Capstone Courses and Projects 145
Motivating Students to Learn with Project-Based Learning 146
The Power of Reflection: The 'Thought-Piece' in Capstone Courses 148
Preparing Preservice Teachers for the edTPA: Frustrations
 and Tips for Teacher Educators 151
Effective Utilization of a Capstone Project: A Case Study Oral Exam 154
Using Graduate-Level Action Research to Impact Teacher Effectiveness
 and Student Achievement 156
From Paper to Social Networking: Updating Capstone Assignments
 for the Electronic Age 157

X. ePortfolios 163
Six-Word Stories—A Simple, Powerful Portfolio Reflection Tool 164
ePortfolios as a Multidimensional Learning Experience
 for Preservice Teachers 168
ePortfolios Help Students Integrate Their Learning 170

Afterword 175

About the Authors 177

Preface

When we looked back through the Prefaces of the past few books in the "It Works for Me Series," we discovered that we had opened them by writing about instances in our past when we either employed the subject or wrote essays about it (e.g., SOTL). Interestingly, one of the points we make in those Prefaces is that back then we didn't employ metacognitive or SoTL principles purposefully. Like a lot of teachers who have been around awhile, we (especially Hal and Charlie) sometimes stumble into the subject without having done the research, but one reason for writing this book is to convince you to utilize high impact practices (HIPs) **intentionally**.

High impact practices are a twenty-first-century phenomenon, but if you've read any of our books, you know, for instance, that for many years we have been collaborating, instructing undergraduates how to research like full professors, and, since our major discipline is English, teaching writing intensive courses—in short, employing some high impact practices, even though, back then, they were merely effective teaching strategies.

What impresses us the most about HIPs is that they have been rigorously assessed, and no doubt remains that they work, resulting in deeper learning. Moreover what started as a top ten practices list has already grown to eleven with the demonstrated efficacy of the e-portfolio. And that list will surely grow as more and more research is performed.

If we were to push for the 12th HIP, we would probably advocate for **mentorships**. During this semester every Friday morning, we have been co-facilitating—another form of collaboration—a professional learning community (PLC) on the scholarship of teaching and learning, our last "It Works for Me" subject. What we primarily discovered were three things that helped our PLC participants the most:

1. **Mentors**. Participants thrived under the system we established whereby each of the three facilitators met on a weekly basis with four participants and remained available during the week. Of course, the reason the mentoring worked so well was that it incorporated some traits that Kuh believes permeate all of the high impact practices—frequent, timely, and constructive feedback; high-level performance expectations (participants had to write a publishable article); a significant investment of time and effort over an extended period of time; and interactions with faculty and peers (importantly, while HIPs are aimed at students, they work equally well for faculty learning).

2. **Collaboration**. Using ourselves as examples, we encouraged participants to collaborate if not on full articles, on shared research and editing.
3. **Disciplined Approach**. Our teacher-scholars were shown that their chances for publication improved if they could carve a daily schedule out of their time, write in a specific place, and set themselves a word-count goal in the beginning.

Note, however, that none of our suggestions is truly evidence-based, and the plural of anecdote is never evidence. As a result, we have been collecting as much evidence as we can to prove out point.

Our PLC brings up another important point we need to stress: **No law exists that prevents you from using more than one HIP at a time in a learning experience**. In fact, as our PLC experience proved, piggybacking the HIPs makes them even more effective, or, as Mae West said, "Too much of a good thing can be . . . wonderful."

We hope you find the tips in this book the same way . . . wonderful.

An Introduction To High-Impact Practices (HIPs)

A Brief Overview

Until Dumbledore's Elder Wand is located, the most effective method for teaching and learning lies in the utilization of high-impact practices. According to George Kuh (2008, Kuh & O'Donnell 2013) and colleagues at the Association of American Colleges and Universities (AAC&U), high impact practices promote deep learning, increase the rates in student engagement as well as retention, and aid historically underserved student populations. Kuh identified ten active learning practices that fulfill his definition, and recently an eleventh practice was added:

- First-Year Seminars and Experiences
- Common Intellectual Experiences
- Learning Communities
- Writing-Intensive Courses
- Collaborative Assignments and Projects
- Undergraduate Research
- Diversity/Global Learning
- Service Learning, Community-Based Learning
- Internships
- Capstone Courses and Projects
- ePortfolios.

Kuh also offered some stipulations and reasons for the success of the HIPs. To engage students at high levels, Kuh argues, it is not enough just to employ one of the eleven, but "these practices must be done well." Kuh further explains certain important traits permeate the practices, making them high-impact:

- performance expectations set at appropriately high levels
- significant investment of time and effort by students over an extended period of time
- interactions with faculty and peers about substantive matters
- experience with diversity

- frequent timely, and constructive feedback
- periodic, structured opportunities to reflect and integrate learning
- opportunities to discover relevance of learning through real-world applications
- public demonstration of competence.

Some Timely Tips for Applying HIPs

Kuh, the founding director of the National Survey of Student Engagement (NSSE), recommends that institutions create ways for their students to participate in at least two HIPs during their undergraduate experience, one during their first year and one during the context of their major. While students can be required to take such items as a writing-intensive course and encouraged to participate in such activities as Study Abroad and internships, professors and departments can also adjust their pedagogies, curricula, and individual courses to include some of the eleven HIPs and eight important traits.

Our university asked us to construct a list of tips that faculty members interested in utilizing HIPs could apply to their classes. Obviously, any instructor could start with Kuh's eight traits—a high bar, significant effort, frequent interactions between the instructor and class members, multiple feedback opportunities, periodic reflection, real-world assignments, and public demonstrations through reading and speaking—and incorporate them into his/her classes. In addition, we offered these suggestions:

1. First-Year Seminars may not work for every major, but the key elements found in these courses can be included in all first-year courses: critical inquiry, frequent writing, information literacy, and collaborative learning.

2. Common Intellectual Experiences, or a core curriculum, already exist because of the University's Quality Enhancement Plan (QEP). As a result, all classes should be undergirded by any of its strategies.

3. Any campus unit can establish learning communities. Departments are encouraged to link courses so that knowledge, skills, and strategies build upon each other, often by following the Revised Bloom's Taxonomy (2001) so that lower-division courses stress lower-order thinking while upper-division courses emphasize higher-order thinking.

4. According to Arum and Roksa's *Academically Adrift*, (2011), too many students do not write papers in their courses, especially long, in-depth papers (their recommendation is for twenty-plus-page papers). Instructors are encouraged to assure their students engage in in-depth writing.

5. Instructors should make certain their active-learning pedagogy includes collaboration both in class and outside of class, even in their written work. Collaboration can be student-student or even student-instructor.

6. While every assigned paper need not be pure research, during the semester every instructor can assign at least one, stressing such skills as formulating a research question/hypothesis/thesis, developing a review of relevant literature, qualitative reasoning, quantitative reasoning, and appropriate documentation.

7. Faculty can emphasize the importance of perspective shift, wherein students are asked to view an idea, situation, or experience from multiple positions.

8. Many courses contain, if not a service-learning component, a community-based component.

9. Faculty and departments are encouraged to investigate possible internships in their field and to urge students to participate in these internships.

10. Every major needs a capstone experience. ePortfolios provide a way of conducting such courses either completely online or in some hybrid format.

11. Instructors are encouraged to set the bar high but not out of reach.

12. Instructors should provide sufficient work to push students beyond their study-discovered habit of studying only five total hours per week during the entire semester.

13. Faculty should search for opportunities to create interactions with students beyond class time. Faculty-student collaboration on research affords an excellent method. Encouraging student study groups and providing collaborative assignments also foster peer collaboration.

14. Faculty members who demonstrate inclusion and diversity provide a model for their students.

15. Faculty need to include a statement in their syllabi that feedback on assignments will be frequent, timely, and constructive, then follow through on this commitment.

16. Faculty are encouraged to provide both in-class and out-of-class opportunities for students to reflect upon and thus monitor their own learning. The five-minute reflection paper serves as an appropriate instrument for almost every class.

17. When possible, faculty can assign homework, papers, and projects that relate to real-world learning.

18. Faculty can provide class time for student presentations of papers and projects as well as encouraging submission for presentation/publication of key undergraduate work.

Previous Books

Just as you are probably discovering that you have been employing HIPs throughout your career, especially the eight traits Kuh identifies, so we find we have written about a lot of them. Our *Achieving Excellence in Teaching* (2014) covers many of the

Kuh traits. *It Works for Us, Collaboratively* (2006) covers various tactics one can use in collaborative research and writing and even includes a section on faculty-student collaboration. Likewise, our *It Works for Me as a Scholar-Teacher* (2008) devotes half the book to "Enhancing Your Students' Scholarship," emphasizing effective methodologies as well as how to foster collaborations. Just as the HIPs cut across so much of academia, so do our books.

The Plan of This Book

When we sent out the call for submissions to this book, we observed another cut-across. We asked contributors to provide a label for each tip as to which HIP was covered, and we discovered that in some cases, more than one HIP was announced. As we read over some of the HIPs, we noticed that—even when only one HIP was listed—the tip was applied across several HIPs. For organizational purposes, we have arranged the body of this book by the essay's primary HIP, but we encourage you to ascertain whether the advice could apply to other HIPs as well. Kuh's assertion of the eight common traits found in the HIPs likewise suggests such an application could be embedded in the advice.

As we perused the submissions for this book, we found one glaring omission that we don't understand. No one submitted a tip about learning communities. Is that because professional learning communities have become such a successful strategy for professors that applying the principles to students is not considered? We find it difficult to believe that instructors, groups of instructors, programs, and majors are not using student-oriented learning communities. Twenty years ago Hal and Charlie published an article about how they converted their upper-division writing classes into triads of writers in similar genres (e.g., serious/literary fiction, romance, mystery/thrillers, and sci fi/fantasy), and for the twenty years before that they had discovered how effective small communities of students with similar interests could be. In fact, as we type this intro, we know of two of those original triads still surviving. Likewise, their Fall 2007 article on "Modeling the Writing Assignment on Literature" (*Eureka Studies in Teaching Short Fiction*, 8(1), 139-146) details how triads can be used to generate undergraduate scholarship in upper-division American lit courses.

For those of you who love statistics, here is a breakdown by HIP type and number of the published submissions (i.e., our distribution list):
- Collaborative Assignments and Projects: 15
- Diversity and Global Learning: 10
- Undergraduate Research: 7
- Service/Community-Based Learning: 6

- Capstones: 6
- Writing-Intensive Courses: 4
- ePortfolios: 3
- Common Intellectual Experiences: 3
- Internships: 3
- First-Year Seminars and Experiences: 2.

Charge

Now that we have primed the pump with some HIPs Tips, we are turning this book over to some of our country's best teacher-scholars. It's our belief that every class taught can be infused with some HIPs wisdom and therefore become more effective. What follows will give you some food for thought, so as Mom used to tell us, "Clean your plate."

I. First-Year Seminars and Experiences

The following are characteristics of this HIP:
- Small groups of students meet with faculty regularly.
- A strong emphasis is placed on: critical inquiry, frequent writing, literacy, and collaborative learning.
- Faculty involve students with cutting-edge questions in scholarship and with the faculty members' own research.

This section contains two articles. Can you suggest the essentials of a first-year program for school's wishing to create this experience?

What Factors Make First-year Undergraduate Experiences Successful?

Before I [Annie] started my first year at my undergraduate university, I have to admit I was nervous. My main worries ran the gamut of concerns, couched under two big fears: *How am I going to make friends? Will I be able to succeed academically?* When I arrived on campus, I was introduced to my orientation group where I immediately made social connections. We connected through some similar life experiences, but mostly we bonded over the tasks we had to complete during our three-day weekend camping experience. When I returned to campus and began classes, all first-year students were enrolled in a specific class, the Freshman Focus, with a professor who would serve not only as our teacher, but as our advisor. My classmates in the Freshman Focus class grew together through group projects and service projects, discussing our triumphs and failures during that first semester. I remain close friends with many individuals from those groups today. However, I noticed that not all orientation groups were as successful as mine were, including some of these classes at the same university. In fact, many students from other groups dropped out of school or transferred. This situation made me wonder, what factors make first-year experiences successful?

Peer education and leadership is a widely used academic success strategy in higher education institutions. Latino and Unite (2012) suggest that peer facilitation plays a critical role in first-year seminars. Peer facilitators have many benefits as they are cost-effective, readily available, and often less intimidating to students than professors. Peer educators can provide a unique perspective for first-time college students, as well as address the similar issues frequently faced by students transitioning into college. In fact, peer facilitators often become lasting resources and systems of support as students progress through their undergraduate studies. In my Freshman Focus class, we had an older student who served as a resource to answer questions we didn't feel comfortable asking our professor. I frequently used our peer facilitator as a source of support until graduation. Thus, one key element of successful first-year experiences is peer mentoring.

Another helpful first-year experience intervention is encouraging students to examine their own values. A 2016 article by Danitz, Suvak, and Orsillo examined the effects of an Acceptance-Based Behavioral Workshop with first-year undergraduate students. The authors found that depression levels decreased in first-year students who participated in the workshop as compared to those students in a control group. In my personal experience, our class incorporated various activities to self-explore values at the beginning, middle, and end of the semester, and we frequently discussed our values with our professor and classmates. This constant focus on values and goals is consistent with best practices. Using acceptance and values work may be beneficial in helping first-year students form their own identities, a vital task in college, particularly as students continue to grow and develop through their late teens and early twenties (Arnett, 2000).

Finding a social group and sharing new experiences with peers seems to have a positive effect on first-year students as well. In a 2010 qualitative study, Maunder, Gingham, and Rogers conducted semi-structured interviews with first and second year undergraduates to explore themes of early college experiences. They found that most students cited a need for a social group with others similar to them as foundational to success in college. Specifically, finding a social group as a sort of safe base helped reduce anxiety, and students felt freer to explore and develop their own individual identities. A second theme identified was students' need to know what to expect from the college experience. Students reported that hearing from other college students about how to succeed and what to expect in college was vital to their development. Older students were valued by younger ones for being able to share both their high and low moments, as well as their "A-ha" experiences. In short, to be successful, first-year students need a roadmap of how to navigate the uncharted waters of college.

First-year seminars and experiences are becoming more commonplace in many universities, but not all of them are equally effective at reaching their goals of student growth, learning, bonding, and retention. As a result, researchers are increasingly trying to determine which aspects of first-year experiences most contribute to student success. Overall, research supports building connections with older peers, developing close and ongoing faculty mentorship and advising, facilitating peer-to-peer relationships, as well as helping students explore their values. These simple techniques are the most research-supported interventions in creating meaningful first-year experiences for students.

References

Arnett, J.J. (2000). Emerging adulthood: A theory of development from the late teens through the twenties. *American Psychologist, 55*(5), 469-480.

Danitz, S.B., Suvak, M.K., & Orsillo, S.M. (2016). The mindful way through the semester: Evaluating the impact of integrating an acceptance-based behavioral program into a first-year experience course for undergraduates. *Behavior Therapy, 47*(4), 487-499.

Latino, J.A., & Unite, C.M. (2012). Providing academic support through peer education. *New Directions for Higher Education, 157*, 31-43.

Maunder, R.E., Gingham, J., & Rogers, J. (2010) Transition in higher education: Exploring the experiences of first and second year psychology undergraduate students. *The Psychology of Education Review, 34*(1), 50-54.

Annie Baumer, Spalding University
Nardin Michaels, Spalding University

"OMG!" – An Orientation to Media Genres for College Freshmen

The difficulties that freshmen face during their first semester in college can be extremely challenging. Research by scholars like Moffatt (1989) illustrate how hard it is for these students to adjust to the teaching styles of their professors and establish the amount of time they must spend studying. Erickson and Strommer (1991) point out that it is critical for beginning college freshmen to develop realistic expectations for their performance to avoid stress. In addition, Guskey (1988) emphasizes how important it is for freshmen students to experience some form of successful academic achievement to increase their chances of staying in college. As these students face this kind of adversity, it's important to expose them to a first-year seminar course that teaches them how to transform their use of media for the purposes of entertainment into their use of media for the purposes of enhancing their academic performance. For the last 5 years, I have taught a class called "OMG"– an abbreviation for the course titled "An Orientation to Media Genres"--to first-semester freshmen at Otterbein University. A course like this gives professors a chance to help freshmen adapt to college life by getting them to strategically use traditional media like books, film, television, and radio to help them improve their academic performance. In addition, students can also learn how to use critical thinking to identify, critique, and navigate the misleading information often found on social media sites. Equally important is the opportunity to explore relatively newer media platforms like podcasting for academic enrichment.

In my experience teaching this freshman seminar, I have found it useful to become familiar with the general media use patterns of my students as media consumers. Knowledge of how students use media helps professors make informed decisions about facilitating classroom discussions and incorporating relatable examples. A good way to get an impression of this situation is to look at Nielsen's report (2016) examining media use activity. It describes some typical media use patterns of people in the age category of 18-34 years. The average amount of weekly time spent consuming all-media platforms is 26 hours and 49 minutes. 6 hours and 19 minutes of that time is spent on social media. During a typical week, 78% of people within this age group prefer to spend their time on social media with their smart phone devices. 10% of adults within this age group prefer to spend their time on social media using a tablet. And the other 12% of adults within this age group prefer to spend their time on social media using a PC. Their most popular social media platforms are Facebook, Instagram, Twitter, and Pinterest. In addition, the Pew Research Center (2016) conducted a news consumer study for adults between the ages of 18-29. It revealed that 50% of them prefer to get their news on-line. 27% of the people in this group prefer to get their news from regular television. 14% prefer to get their news from radio. And 5% prefer to get their news from print media.

During the semester, I have the students complete several projects and assignments that fit Kuh and O'Donnell's (2013) definition of High Impact Learning practices. For this contribution, I will explain how I utilize the "Common Intellectual Experience" for my students. A significant part of the class is organizing lessons about media around the university's annual common book lecture. Each year, all incoming freshmen students are provided a copy of a popular book selected by a university committee. They are required to write an essay about the book before they come to the first-class meeting. Previous common book authors included Rebecca Skloot, the author of *The Immortal Life of Henrietta Lacks* (2010) and Bryan Stevenson, the author of *Just Mercy* (2014). Since the book is one of the oldest forms of media used in education, it provides a good starting point for this class. Other forms of media then become relevant. Rebecca Skloot's book was eventually produced as a movie for HBO. Bryan Stevenson's book referenced a *60 Minutes* story featuring the case of one of his clients on death row. These examples show that the stories from each book can produce alternate media versions which creates new paths of inquiry to pursue in class. Since books provide some of the most in-depth stories, there is usually an opportunity to get students reflecting on how important media use is to the plot. For instance, when students had to read the book *Running the Rift* by author Naomi Benaron (2012), (a fictional account of the Rwandan Genocide conflict between the Hutu and Tutsi tribes), it gave me a chance to facilitate a conversation about how the book depicted the country's reliance on radio as the main source of information. This strategy led to an insightful classroom discussion about media use in different cultures. It also provided an opportunity to show students a documentary called "Finding Hillywood" (Towey and Warshawski, 2013). The documentary showed how Rwandans who survived the devastating conflict began to produce films reflecting their experience. They traveled to different parts of the country to show their work through a film festival. This common intellectual experience culminates when the author of the common book visits the campus and gives a lecture about the book. All the students are required to attend the lecture, which usually includes many chances to interact with the author. In preparation for the visit, my students are required to write a series of inquisitive questions based on their reaction to the book and our discussions in class.

Overall, the common book experiences have allowed me as a professor to emphasize the value of diversity and global education through the topics that are dealt with in each book. They have allowed me to emphasize information literacy through the sources that each author cites to ensure that their work is credible. They have also allowed me to emphasize a sense of morality because each story encourages our students to reflect on some form of social responsibility.

References

Benaron, N. (2012). *Running the rift.* Chapel Hill, N.C: Algonquin Books.

Erickson, B.L., & Strommer, D.W. (1991). *Teaching college freshmen.* San Francisco: Jossey-Bass.

Guskey, T.R., (1988). *Improving student learning in college classrooms.* Springfield, IL: Charles C. Thomas Publishers

Kuh, G.D., & O'Donnell, K. (2013). *Ensuring quality and taking high impact practices to scale.* Washington, D.C.: AAC&U.

Moffatt, M. (1989). *Coming of age in New Jersey.* New Brunswick, N.J.: Rutgers University Press.

Nielsen, (2016). *2016 Nielsen Social Media Report.* Retrieved August 13, 2017 from http://www.nielsen.com/us/en/insights/reports/2017/2016-nielsen-social-media-report.html

Pew Research Center. (2016, July 7). *Pathways to News.* Retrieved August 13, 2017 from http://www.journalism.org/2016/07/07/pathways-to-news/.

Skloot, R. (2010). *The immortal life of Henrietta Lacks.* New York: Crown Publishing Group.

Stevenson, B. (2014). *Just mercy: A story of justice and redemption.* New York: Spiegel & Grau.

Towey, C. (Co-Director), Warshawski, L. (Co-Director). (2013). *Finding hillywood* [Documentary]. Rwanda: Inflatable Film.

Eric K. Jones, Otterbein University

II. Common Intellectual Experiences

The following are characteristics of this HIP:
- A set of common courses or vertically organized general education program is required.
- Experiences involve advanced integrative studies and/or participation in a learning community.
- Experiences usually combine broad themes with a variety of curricular/cocurricular options.

This section contains three articles. What would you consider the most important theme for students in these experiences to use as a focus?

Picture This

Common Intellectual Experiences

For many educators, Madeline Hunter and her theories of Mastery Teaching have run their course. Madeline, however, left me with an eternal truth that *teachers must establish interest first for any lesson if they expect students to become engaged with the content*. This truth is a common intellectual experience for a kindergarten class identifying shapes or a Ph.D. Class analyzing organizational behavior. Linked to this first reality is that *Everyone likes to be read to regardless how old they are*. For the past sixteen years, I have taught a doctoral program, preparing school leaders, P20. Here is how, at even a doctoral level of sophistication and aptitude, we can grab student interest and shape motivation throughout our lesson.

A course I teach at the University is called Organizational Analysis for Educational Leadership. Three critical objectives for the course guide instruction: develop an appreciation of organizational theory, describe the influence of the political economy of educational settings and analyze regulatory processes and application. These objectives represent high-level academic expectations. However, doctorate-level coursework does not have to take itself so seriously. I have found that starting class by reading a child's picture book to my doctorate students draws interest, connects their thinking to the lesson outcomes, requires little of them except listening to and enjoying a story, and for a few moments, places them outside an adult world into that of a child.

Captivating interest for a subject is critical for meaningful instruction, but remember that establishing lesson objectives must be an early priority before opening any picture book. The Cheshire cat, in Carroll's *Alice's Adventures in Wonderland*, explains that if Alice doesn't know where she wants to go, then it doesn't matter which direction she takes. With teaching, having direction assures a destination. Without establishing a destination first, we are just reading a picture book ignoring any promise of where we are taking students. That would be "madness" as the Cheshire cat will tell us. Below are a couple of examples of how I have used picture books to set my lesson objectives.

In an organizational analysis course, we examine problems of practice and the intricacies of thought around their solutions. Students read chapters from Bolman and Deal's (2013) *Reframing Organizations*, Dirkx's (2006) *Studying the Complicated Matter of What Works*, and Jordan, Kleinsasser, and Roe's (2014) *Wicked problems: Inescapable Wickedity*. Before we unpack the independent reading and explore the various avenues to organizational problem solving, I read to them Kobi Yamada's *What Do You Do with a Problem?* The story of a little boy's journey to discover that problems are ways we learn, engages them. We return to essential elements of the picture book as we work through the presentation.

The Numberlys, by William Joyce, offers another picture book example. Introducing qualitative methods and their place in scholarship, this book follows a community of Numberlys who are quite comfortable in a world where numbers prevailed. They live in a world without books, jellybeans, or pizza. Suddenly, pieces of numbers fall from the machinery to form letters and later colorful words. The book uses color to build a contrast between the gray structures of numbers and the bright, color-crafted shapes of letters and words. The distinction may be stark, but it helps draw a contrast between research that controls and predicts and research which recognizes multiple realities and questions assumptions. Students often reject quantitative approaches as too touchy-feely and lack empirical certainty. *The Numberlys* starts a conversation, exploring multiple realities and alternative strategies for understanding problems.

Picture books offer simple perspectives on complex issues. Hunter makes this important, enduring assertion "[The] way we can make the material more interesting is by accentuating the novel or vivid." Introducing a child's world to adult thinking makes the complex "novel" and the ill-defined "vivid."

References

Bolman, L. G., & Deal, T. E. (2013). Reframing organizations: Artistry, choice and leadership (5th ed.). San Francisco, CA: Jossey-Bass.

Carroll, L. (1999). *Alice's adventures in wonderland.* Cambridge, MA: Candlewick Press.

Dirkx, J. M. (2006). Studying the complicated matter of what works: Evidence-based research and the problem of practice. *Adult Education Quarterly,* 56(4) 273-290. doi: 10.1177/0741713606289358

Hunter, M. (1982). *Mastery teaching: Increasing instructional effectiveness in elementary, secondary schools, colleges and universities.* Thousand Oaks, CA: Corwin Press.

Jordan, M. E, Kleinsasser, R. C. & Roe, M. (2014). Wicked problems: Inescapable wickedity. *Pedagogy,* 40(4), 415-430.

Joyce, W. (2014). *The numberlys.* New York, NY: Moonbot Books.

Yamada, K. (2016) *What do you do with a problem*? Seattle, WA: Compendium Inc.

Paul Watkins, Southeast Missouri State University

Using the Deathly Hallows: Combining High-Impact Practices for First-Year Success

HIPs Addressed: Common Intellectual Experiences, Collaborative Assignments/Projects, Writing-Intensive Courses

In J.K. Rowling's *Harry Potter* series, Harry spends the final novel preparing for a battle with the evil wizard Voldemort. In order to emerge victorious, he must collect the following items: the Resurrection Stone, which can bring back the dead; the Invisibility Cloak, which can hide any soul from Death itself; and the Elder Wand, which, in the right hands, can defeat any wizard in a duel. Together, these items create a force strong enough to destroy any evil and to allow the boy wizard to escape the battle unscathed. "Together, the Deathly Hallows," a friend tells Harry, "if united, will make the possessor Master of Death" (Rowling, 2007, pp. 409-410). I believe that High-Impact Practices (Kuh, 2008) are the Deathly Hallows of the classroom, affording instructors impeccable protection from failure and hardship—and, when joined together, make them the "Master of Death" in their own classrooms.

As instructors, we now have to work harder than ever to combat the collective mindset of our new generation of students. The iGen, as they have been dubbed by scholars (e.g., Twenge, 2017), are addicted to technology and uninterested in educational traditions. A typical lecture-style class bores them, and they want access to technology (and the instant gratification it offers) during class time (Twenge, 2017). They also have more practical goals in the classroom and no longer believe in pursuing education for its own sake. Fitting within the "student-as-consumer" (SAC) model of education, iGen students are much more focused on the "consumer experience" (Molesworth, Nixon, & Scullion, 2009, p. 279) of getting a college degree that is more focused on preparing for the workplace and less on the acquisition of general knowledge. This mindset, to further the Harry Potter metaphor, is our Voldemort in the classroom; it threatens to destroy our livelihood as protectors of knowledge in the Ivory Tower and changes the world as academics know it. It is our job to show our students that a college education does not have to be an either/or situation when it comes to real-world applications and general knowledge, to convince them that education (and not skill acquisition) can make a difference in their lives. We can become Masters of Death in higher education by engaging our iGen students in a quality educational experience by instituting high-impact practices in our classrooms. Allow me to suggest one way we might go about it.

At the University of Kentucky, I belong to a cohort of instructors who teach CIS 110, an introductory communication and composition class that is part of UK's general education coursework (UK Core). CIS 110 which offers students the chance to hone both their public speaking and writing skills, is structured around three major speeches and two essay assignments. Instructors receive only the bare bones of the course—a schedule of lessons and due dates, an online classroom, and assignment rubrics—and it is entirely up to them to create engaging and informative lessons, using whatever formats and tools they like. As a first-time instructor, I chose to employ the high-impact common intellectual experiences, writing-intensive courses, and collaborative assignments/projects practices—my Deathly Hallows, if you will—to ensure a successful first semester of teaching.

First, CIS 110 is a *common intellectual experience* for more than 1,000 students at the University of Kentucky. Students in the course are typically paired up with students from members of their respective colleges, helping to solidify not only the intellectual but also social bonds among students. This cohort-style course placement, along with the small class size (capped at 25 students per section), creates "learning communities" (Kuh, 2008, para. 4) within the classroom that support learning across all disciplines. My students, largely pursuing majors in the health sciences, formed a community in my class that later led to the creation of study groups for anatomy exams and communal lunches to gripe about chemistry. Their end-of-course reflection videos highlighted their appreciation for this experience: "I really enjoyed getting to know my classmates," one student said, "because they've become some of my best friends on campus."

This creation of a community, though partly influenced by the course's place in the UK Core, was also intentional on my part. I wanted my students to have the opportunity to engage in *collaborative assignments and projects* throughout the course. Each class consisted of at least one group activity, through which students would apply course material to the real world as well as "learn to work in the company of others" (Kuh, 2008, para. 7). My students created event posters to target different audiences during an audience analysis lesson, cited sources during an in-class *Amazing Race* when learning to use APA style, and went on a group scavenger hunt for academic articles to practice finding and evaluating sources. I also turned one of their "impromptu speech" days into a group impromptu day, where students worked together to pitch health-related TV episodes based on information from the CDC's Entertainment Education website and argued for which restaurant we should add to the campus dining options. These activities were cited again and again amongst course evaluations as the students' favorite parts of CIS 110, as they allowed students time to build community *and* apply the course material—rather than just listen to lectures for 50 minutes at a time, as we know the iGens deplore.

Finally, CIS 110 offers students the chance to take a *writing-intensive course* they might not otherwise take as part of their major coursework. My students wrote two papers—an analysis of a speech (3 pages) and an informative essay on a topic of their choice (5 pages)—with opportunities to revise their work throughout both writing processes. In crafting our semester schedule, the CIS 110 course director built in five days for revisions and proofreading during our semester. My students revised and resubmitted their public speaking analyses based on my feedback within the first month of the semester; later, students revised each other's informative essay drafts and even offered feedback on each other's final speech outlines. Once again, these activities were cited as student favorites in course evaluations: "The revisions were helpful," one student wrote, "because they made my writing better and helped bring up my grade."

None of these practices, however, would have worked without the others. I would not have taught a *writing-intensive course* without opportunities for my students to engage with one another's work, nor would these *collaborative assignments and projects* work without the creation of a classroom community, which would not have existed without the *common intellectual experience* of the UK Core. And so it goes. I believe that, just like Harry Potter discovers in *Deathly Hallows*, solutions to problems can be far simpler (and far more connected) than we ever imagined. After all, Harry becomes Master of Death only by connecting his three weapons "together"—using the Deathly Hallows to overcome any obstacle that comes his way.

And if it can work for Harry Potter, it can work for us, too.

References

Kuh, G.D. (2008). High-impact educational practices. *Association of American Colleges and Universities*. Retrieved from https://www.aacu.org/leap/hips

Molesworth, M., Nixon, E., & Scullion, R. (2009). Having, being and higher education: The marketisation of the university and the transformation of the student into consumer. *Teaching in Higher Education, 14*(3), 277-287. http://dx.doi.org/10.1080/13562510902898841

Rowling, J.K. (2007). *Harry Potter and the deathly hallows*. New York: Scholastic.

Twenge, J. (2017). *iGen: Why today's super-connected kids are growing up less rebellious, more tolerant, less happy—and completely unprepared for adulthood, and what that means for the rest of us*. New York, NY: Simon & Schuster.

Hayley C. Hoffman, University of Kentucky

Improving Course Plans Via Standardized Committee Review

Our department divides oversight of course syllabi across several curriculum committees. Recently, all these committees were additionally tasked with reviewing individual instructors' course plans as part of an alignment toward improved assessment practices. This review process was designed to help faculty align their course plans—the individual instructor's plans for a section of the course—to the department's official syllabus, which specifies the required topics, learning outcomes, and assessments. We hoped to catch potential pitfalls or missing elements in the process. A clear course plan ensures that students are being given an accurate idea of how the course will serve the stated learning objectives.

We both serve on the Foundations Curriculum Committee, which is responsible for freshman- and sophomore-level courses taken by majors and minors. We reviewed the study by Stanny, Gonzalez, and McGowan (2015) about assessing the culture of teaching and learning by reviewing course plans, and we could see how its goals and outcomes aligned with the responsibilities of our committee. We realized we could use their results as a starting point to develop a process that would provide the required review of course plans while also potentially improving the culture of learning within the department: by our providing constructive feedback to faculty about their plans before the semester starts, they will have an opportunity to improve their plans before actually providing it to the students. Indirectly, it is our hope that—over time—the faculty will review the list of items we did not find in their plans and consider adding them to their course. Thus, the learning environment in our courses would improve.

We created a simple form in Google Docs through which committee members could review submitted course plans. The form consists of four sections, starting with basic administrative information, such as course number, semester and year, and the instructor's name. The second section lists items that are required by college policy, such as grading and attendance policies. The two additional sections provide a list of best-practices and high-impact practices inspired by Stanny, Gonzalez, and McGowan (2015). These two sections are primarily pedagogical items rather than administrative. For example, in the consideration of best practices, we evaluate whether a course plan includes descriptions of specific projects and expected technology skills; the section on High-Impact Practices covers the educational practices described by Kuh (2008). For each item, the form allows a response of "yes," "no," and "other/see below," and the form concludes with an additional free text response area.

Roughly a week before each semester begins, we send an e-mail to the faculty teaching one of the courses for which the committee is responsible, asking them to send us a copy of their course plan. In the e-mail, we provide a PDF copy of the form we will be using, and explain that we will review their course plans against the items on the form and promptly provide feedback to them. When we receive a response, a committee member uses the form to evaluate the plan, looking for the presence of the administrative items as well as evidence of the pedagogical items listed in the best practices and high-impact practices sections. Once complete, we use the Google Forms to capture a PDF report of our assessment, which is promptly returned to the faculty member. Individual reviews generally take less than half an hour, sometimes much less if it is a course plan reviewed in a previous semester.

This course review is not yet mandatory; the committee does not have the authority to enforce such a policy if there were one. However, we have received 50-75% compliance with our review requests for each of the four regular semesters we have been conducting these evaluations. This high rate of compliance may be in part because these courses are primarily taught by adjunct faculty who are generally willing to participate in such standardized assessments. Several instructors have reported making changes to their course plans based on our reviews, including both editorial changes to improve the plan's clarity as well as pedagogic changes to improve the course's effectiveness.

We have found this review of course plans takes negligible time each semester, since we spread the work amongst the committee members. It appears to be making a positive impact on the quality of the course plans being provided to our students. Perhaps most importantly, we see evidence that we are planting seeds in faculty's minds about implementing more of the best practices and high-impact practices in future semesters.

References

Kuh, G. D. (2008). *High-Impact educational practices: What they are, who has access to them, and why they matter*: AAC&U.

Stanny, C., Gonzalez, M., & McGowan, B. (2015). Assessing the culture of teaching and learning through a syllabus review. *Assessment & Evaluation in Higher Education, 40*(7), 898-913. doi:10.1080/02602938.2014.956684

Paul Gestwicki, Ball State University
David L. Largent, Ball State University

III. Writing-Intensive Courses

The following are characteristics of this HIP:
- Writing is found from first-year to final-year courses.
- The focus is on writing for different audiences in different disciplines.
- Students learn the entire process from idea generation through final revision.

This section contains four articles. Is writing important in your discipline? Is there any course you teach in which you don't require writing? If so, how could you incorporate the writing process into your syllabi?

Developing Scientific Thinking Through Writing

I [Dede] begin this essay by sharing a confession: *I don't really know what the word "rhetoric" means.* So, as colleagues and I met (once again) to determine the best way to teach writing to our students as part of a university-wide initiative, I mostly nodded agreeably, especially when the word "rhetoric" was mentioned by my colleagues in the English department. Over time, the plan coalesced around how we would teach students to become better writers. The plan expanded and then was simplified, like a living and breathing being, its major themes clearer with each revision, eventually becoming almost lyrical in its elegance. The team rejoiced in the final masterpiece: a university-wide plan to build writing-intensive courses across the curriculum.

Optimistically, we took the plan to the campus science building, confident that we could convince even the most reluctant chemists, physicists, and mathematicians that writing had a role in their classrooms. The meeting was hard on many levels: the professors represented hard sciences, which made it a hard sell without hard data. We left the meeting defeated, with a realization that without the "right" kind of support that would be viewed as legitimate by our scientific colleagues, our plan would sit idle. We scoured the literature and found our justification, which is summarized below:

- Critical thinking develops when students are asked to solve "ill-structured problems," including asking students to develop a "best solution" to solving a messy problem, and supporting their hypotheses with reasons and evidence (Kurfiss, 1988). This critical thinking skill is vital to success in both science and math.
- Some of the problems we currently face with leaders and the general public relying on "alternative facts" to support their beliefs stem from gaps in how scientists learn to communicate facts with laypeople. Scientists learning to write clearly and crisply can help alleviate this problem (Kaufman, personal communication, 10/13/17).
- Scientific writing, at its worst, involves "data dumping" in which the writer includes all information s/he has learned about a subject, including meaningless raw data, barely understood statistics, and essentially plagiarized paragraphs because students don't truly and deeply understand the material they are reading. Writing assignments help students deepen their understanding of material by requiring them to assimilate ideas into their own language (Bean, 2011).
- Creating cognitive dissonance is a proven way to dismantle students' inaccurate beliefs about problems. For example, challenging students to write in sup-

port of their thoughts about a widely-believed but inaccurate statement (e.g., Summer is hotter than winter because the sun is closer to the earth) helps students identify erroneous thinking, a foundational step to learning by creating new neurological pathways (Zull, 2002).
- Writing prompts help students understand the "big picture" ideas about a field that are often missed when students get mired in details. For example, asking students a question like, "Chemists often research x and y, yet people rarely ask about z" encourages students' scientific creativity and divergent thinking skills while providing a view of the discipline's key "moves," or ways of thinking (Graff & Birkenstein, 2009).
- Reconsidering writing assignments as *thinking assignments* allows students to see writing as a tool to develop critical thinking necessary to their success as scientists instead of just an isolated skill that is relevant only in their English classes (Bean, 2011).

Finally, to come full circle, let's return to the word *rhetoric*, which has power and applicability far beyond English classes. Rhetoric simply means that students will consider the audience and purpose of their writing (Elbow, 1973), so that they can best assess how their writing can be tailored to their audience so that it is not only heard, but accepted. Said another way, it means that in our approach to the science faculty, we should have considered the audience so that our message was both heard and accepted. Our enthusiasm got us in the door; our conveyance of the purpose (the "why") did not convince our audience. Lesson learned.

Writing as a way to communicate with others is crucial in the hard sciences, for it is what gets emerging ideas shared, manuscripts published, grants awarded, and theses accepted. Even the most skeptical scientist can support those goals.

References

Bean, J.C. (2011). *Engaging ideas: The professor's guide to integrating writing, critical thinking and active learning in the classroom.* San Francisco, CA: Jossey-Bass.

Elbow, P. (1973). *Writing without teachers.* New York, NY: Oxford University Press.

Graff, G. & Birkenstein, C. (2009). *They say/I say: The moves that matter in academic writing* (2nd edition). New York, NY: Norton.

Kurfiss, J.G. Critical thinking: *Theory, research, practice and possibilities. ASHE-ERIC Higher Education Report* (2). Washington, DC.: ERIC Clearinghouse on Higher Education and the Association for the Study of Higher Education as cited in Bean, J.C. (2011), *Engaging ideas: The professor's guide to integrating writing, critical thinking and active learning in the classroom.* San Francisco, CA: Jossey-Bass.

Zull, J.E. (2002). *The art of changing the brain: Enriching the practice of teaching by exploring the biology of learning.* Sterling, VA: Stylus.

DeDe Wohlfarth, Spalding University
Mistalene Calleroz White, Spalding University

A Case of Their Own

For years I've [Robin] provided my students case study books to learn more about the nuances of psychological disorders, family dynamics, etiology, and the many challenges of treatment. My best students enjoy these cases, reading them as if they're a novel. The majority of students, though, are obviously not reading the cases thoroughly as they frequently are unable to answer questions based on the studies. Over the past few years, I have developed a different approach to case studies. I continue to assign a case study book, but I also assign each student to write a 'case of their own.' In a multi-part assignment, students in my child and adolescent abnormal course write their own case studies, including a case history, case conceptualization, and treatment plan.

- Step One: Students select a disorder from a list of possible disorders. The disorders on the list are those we will not have time to address in class and are not reflected in their case study book. It's fine if more than one student selects the same disorder as I do not have students present their work in class.
- Step Two: Students submit a case history similar to the case histories in the case study book required for the course. Basically, case histories are stories about the identified client and their family. The case history should provide necessary details about the identified client – age, gender, race, socioeconomic status, medical history – as well as necessary information about their family of origin, their extended family when appropriate, friends, intimate relationships, school, and extracurricular participation. Finally, the symptoms supporting the diagnosis are interwoven into the case history. Realism counts here, and students are encouraged to include as much detail as necessary. Typically, no scholarly sources are necessary for writing the case history. Case histories tend to run between three and six pages in length.
- Step Three: Students submit a case conceptualization and treatment plan. Once again, students are asked to model their work on the case conceptualization and treatment plan found in the required case study book. In the case conceptualization, students report on what is known about the prevalence/incidence

of the disorder, gender and racial information, and review what is known about the etiology of the disorder. In the treatment plan section, students are asked to review evidence based treatments and a therapist for the case. The selection of the therapist should be based on the nuances of the case and the training of the therapist. Similarly, the treatment section should outline, in detail, the treatment approach selected by the therapist, the factors leading to this decision, and the course of therapy. A realistic appraisal of the factors in the case becomes necessary for students to make appropriate treatment decisions. As might be expected, students must conduct extensive reviews of the scholarly literature to complete this section successfully. In essence, students are conducting all of the research necessary for a term paper on their disorder, but students rarely complain about the level of research needed. Instead, students frequently report that they feel like an expert on their disorder.

- Step Four: Based on instructor feedback, students revise their entire case study and submit it for a final grade. As might be expected, not all students earn A's on this assignment. However, since my asking students to complete this assignment, their understanding of etiology and treatment decision-making has increased.
- Initial Evaluation of Learning from the Assignment: Quiz 1 occurs before students complete step three of this assignment. The average score on etiology and treatment questions on Quiz 1 is consistently in the C range. Prior to my using this assignment, the class average on Quiz 2 and Quiz 3 remained approximately the same for etiology but improved to a B range for treatment. With this assignment, the class average on etiology has risen to a B range as well. Just as importantly, students report enjoying creating their own case study.

Robin K. Morgan, Indiana University Southeast
Nathanael Mitchell, Spalding University

Getting Rid of the Research Paper

In the past, students in my [Robyn] advanced courses completed the standard term or research paper on a topic related to the course. After completing the research and writing the paper, the student submits the paper for my perusal. Of course, as an expert in my field, I don't really need to read another paper on major depression, child sexual abuse, or schizophrenia. Over the past few years, I have created a substitute for this assignment that has led to greater student engagement, higher satisfaction on the part of students with the assignment, and a wider audience for these materials. In addition, I have been able to save my students a couple of hundred dollars by eliminating their purchase of a class textbook. How do I accomplish all of this? Students contribute to a wiki-like, course textbook.

One of my favorite advanced courses is Abnormal Psychology. The students in this course have completed introductory psychology and tend to be juniors or seniors. Most have also completed our Research Methods course, introducing them to American Psychological Association (APA) formatting. I spend approximately two weeks before publishing the online site for my course (we use Canvas at my university, but you can accomplish this task with any learning management system) developing a shell for a course text. Using Canvas pages, I create a title page for my textbook, a table of contents, and links to content pages. I also create the content pages for the first quarter of the course in order to model the type of writing I expect. I create content pages for basic material such as defining what is abnormal, the history of abnormal psychology, theories of abnormality, treatment approaches, ethical issues, and legal considerations. Each of my content pages is formatted in a generally consistent manner using images, tables, figures, paragraphs, and APA formatting for in-text citations. I also create a Reference list page with all references APA formatted.

Students enrolling in the course immediately have access to the textbook from our course site. Students are also immediately assigned one psychological disorder. Using the content page I already created for that disorder, students add information to the content page. Each student adds information about symptoms of the disorder, etiology, and treatment. Students are also able to add case studies, links to outside materials, images, tables, and figures. In-text citations are provided with the full reference added to the References page. Due dates vary from student to student dependent upon which disorder they were assigned. Students assigned disorders addressed earlier in the semester have an earlier due date than students assigned disorders addressed later in the semester. Each new semester, students rewrite one section (e.g., Obsessive Compulsive Disorder) to update the materials.

Student response to this revised writing assignment has been fascinating. Students enjoy seeing their name listed as the author of their section. They especially enjoy knowing that future students will be reading their work (future students add a 'Revised by' with their own name so there is a clear history). On the positive side, this assignment allows students greater flexibility in expressing themselves as they add images, figures, tables, and links to resources. Because of the models provided by the content pages I create, there are fewer problems with APA formatting or writing style than I have encountered in the past on term or research papers. On the negative side, our 'tech-savvy' students are not always so 'tech-savvy.' Detailed instructions about how to add images, tables, figures, and links are necessary. To ensure accessibility of all resources created, careful attention must also be paid to ensuring students add alternative text where required and color choices are consistent. At times, students need assistance determining the accuracy of information they find on websites. However, this situation is no different than helping students who are researching more traditional research papers. In the final analysis, creating a wiki-like course textbook has been a successful approach that helps students to see the importance of what they are writing.

Robin K. Morgan, Indiana University Southeast
Nathanael Mitchell, Spalding University

Writing in the Discipline—Learning the Discourse of Future Professional Communities

Our university subscribes to a Vertical Writing Model (Rhoades & Carroll, 2012) where students take a writing course in each of the four traditional years of study. The first course, taken the freshmen year, explores expository writing, research, and critical thinking more generally. The second course, taken during the sophomore year, exposes students to diverse models of writing expected in different fields of study, including argument, rhetoric, writing studies, and traditional writing across the curriculum. The junior-level writing course is the Writing in the Discipline (WID) course, in which majors focus on the discourse of their specific discipline. Finally, the capstone writing course, taken during the senior year, focuses on advanced level writing within the major with an information literacy component. The focus of this essay will be on the WID course for junior-level Elementary Education majors. More specifically, we will delineate three assignments used in this course and how they are a model for instructors of WID courses wishing to exemplify writing from diverse professional communities.

In accordance with the purpose of a WID course, the mathematics education team at our university developed a series of assignments that mimicked professional writing elementary education teachers are likely to do over the course of their career. In the first assignment, pre-service teachers analyzed a video-taped diagnostic interview of a 2nd grade student who uses three different approaches to solve 70-23—the standard algorithm, base ten blocks, and the hundreds chart (Philipp & Cabral, 2005). She gets different solutions using different strategies. She is puzzled by the inconsistencies among the solutions, but thinks the solution using the traditional algorithm is the correct one. After viewing and discussing the interview in class, the pre-service teachers each write a formal letter to be put in the student's cumulative folder that analyzes the 2nd grade student's use of the three different strategies. The analysis includes, but is not limited to, the mathematical content embedded in each of the solution strategies, inconsistencies in the three strategies, implications for teaching of the student next year in 3rd grade, and how the diagnostic interview helped the pre-service teacher think about their own mathematical knowledge.

The second assignment is a professional development experience that focuses on the nature of and purposes for mathematical tasks in teaching and learning. Prior to engaging in the activity, pre-service teachers read two articles to introduce them to the Math Task Framework (MTF) (Smith & Stein, 1998; Stein & Smith, 1998). During class, the pre-service teachers work with partners to sort a set of subtraction tasks based on the MTF to determine if each task represents a low cognitive demand (LCD) task or a high cognitive demand (HCD) task. The entire class then discusses how and why each group sorted the tasks. Following class, pre-service teachers are instructed to assume they have been assigned by their principal to create a professional development experience for fellow teachers. The overarching goal of the professional development experience is to help pre-service teachers understand the differences between high cognitive demand tasks and low cognitive demand tasks and why it is important to teach using HCD tasks. In a later class, groups exchange the professional development activity with other groups and participate as colleagues. In a reflective paper, the students address how they might adjust their tasks based on how their peers sorted the tasks, modify one of the LCD to a HCD, and delineate the implications for teaching, including an explanation concerning how teaching with LCD and HCD tasks contributes to developing student understanding.

The final assignment in the WID series is a synthesis paper. The students are given the following context: *Your principal comes in to observe your teaching and notes on your evaluation summary that your teaching of double digit subtraction doesn't look like the subtraction he learned. In a written response to the principal, justify the way you are teaching by detailing what you have learned about the content of subtraction.* The justification is a content analysis paper synthesizing evidence of the development of the pre-service teacher's content knowledge of subtraction. The evidence for his/her claims should include: research-based literature (including articles that were read for class and research articles that were found), specific examples from class discussions and experiences, and examinations of curricula including the CCSS goals and objectives.

Naturally, not all WID courses are math and/or education specific, but the activities delineated here are generalizable in the sense of writing examples that imitate the types of professional writing majors will encounter in their future profession. More specifically, our goal with this set of assignments is to expose our pre-service teachers to the diverse ways they will engage in future professional communities. The first assignment is an example of documenting the understanding of a student. It would be similar to any field where one must create an evaluative report on someone s/he supervises. The second assignment demonstrates writing for and with colleagues. In other professions, there would be similar writing experiences, such as reporting on knowledge acquired at professional conferences. The final assignment is an interaction with a supervisor, wherein one creates a written response to an evaluation. Documenting professional interactions with supervisors is an important skill to develop in any profession.

References

Philipp, R. & Cabral, C. (2005). Gretchen Clip Three. IMAP: Integrating Mathematics and Pedagogy to Illustrate Children's Reasoning [Computer software]. San Diego, CA: San Diego University Foundation. Retrieved September 28, 2010. Available from http://www.sci.sdsu.edu/CRMSE/IMAP/main.html

Rhoades, G. & Carroll, B. (2012). Supporting a vertical writing model: Faculty conversations across the curriculum. *Currents in Teaching and Learning, 4*(2), 42-50.

Smith, M. S., & Stein, M. K. (1998). Selecting and creating mathematical tasks: From research to practice. *Mathematics Teaching In The Middle School, 3*(5), 344-50.

Stein, M. K., & Smith, M. S. (1998). Mathematical tasks as a framework for reflection: From esearch to practice. *Mathematics Teaching In The Middle School, 4,* 268-275.

Chrystal Dean, Appalachian State University
Ashley Whitehead, Appalachian State University
Diana Moss, Appalachian State University

IV. Collaborative Assignments and Projects

The following are characteristics of this HIP:
- Collaborating students learn to work with others.
- The insight of collaborating students is sharpened by the process of listening to differing opinions.
- Various types of collaboration are employed, including group work, team-based assignments, and cooperative projects.

This section contains fifteen articles. Even with so many tips, the articles don't exhaust the possibilities for collaboration. Can you come up with some additional possibilities?

How Structured Small Groups (Cooperative Learning) Can Motivate Students

Teachers have for thousands of years worried about students' motivation. Too often, they may ignore their own role in this phenomenon and simply lament, "My students won't work! They are totally uninterested in my subject and would rather play video games." Thanks to cognitive scientists and other researchers, we now know a lot about motivation and the impact teachers can have on it. In fact, as early as 1976 Davidson wrote a paper on the motivation of students in small group learning in mathematics that reflected then-current theories involving cognitive, ego-integrative, and social motives. Now, of course, even more is known about this all-important aspect of teaching.

In a recent publication, Svinicki (2016), for example, makes a key point about motivation: "It is the learner's beliefs and interpretations of what is happening that can make something motivating or not" (p. 1). Thus, teachers must create an environment that gives learners a positive perspective. Their own perspective is not as relevant as their students'.

Environment—which will be the focus of this brief essay—is one of the key four factors that influence motivation. The other factors, according to virtually all modern researchers, including Svinicki, a cognitive psychologist, are goals, values, and expectations.

The importance of goals should come as no surprise to educators. Conscientious teachers identify both course goals and goals for individual units. Such goals, if they are clearly articulated to students can influence their motivation to learn, particularly when they are linked with the two other factors of value and expectancy. Students must believe that the goals are worth attaining; in other words, they must value what they will learn. Instructors can influence students' perceptions that the course goals are worth pursuing. Similarly, they can also help students believe that they can achieve these goals (expectancy).

The classroom environment affects both goals and expectancy as Ambrose, Bridges, Lovett, DiPietro, and Norman (2010) point out. They also note: "If students perceive the environment as supportive . . ., motivation is likely to be enhanced" (p. 79.)

Instructors who care about students' motivation to learn—and that should be all of us—can influence these four factors to differing degrees. Many instructors have found that adopting cooperative learning methods helps them succeed in enhancing students' motivation. Cooperative learning is a highly structured form of group learning that is focused on a task or learning activity suitable for group work. All experts agree that two "givens" distinguish cooperative learning, positive interdependence and individual accountability. First, positive interdependence means that students engage in cooperative, mutually helpful behavior to accomplish a task—often too complex for individual problem solving (Davidson, Major, and Michaelsen, 2014). Secondly, when students are individually accountable, they are responsible for their own learning even though they may work with others to master the material. Other elements that distinguish cooperative learning are group processing—both students and teachers pay attention to what occurs during group work and strive to improve mutual performance—and attention to social and leadership skills such as the ability to draw out group members and shut down dominators. Although it is not a "given," many practitioners of cooperative learning believe in the power of heterogeneity and deliberately create diverse groups (Millis, 2010; Millis and Cottell, 1998).

Cooperative learning probably has its greatest impact on students through the positive environment it creates through mutual interdependence. Human beings have a basic need to affiliate with others. This need can provide a powerful motivational force in the classroom. In small cooperative groups, learning takes place as a shared activity in which each student works closely with a few of her peers. Students exchange ideas freely, ask or answer questions at any time, debate with each other on controversial points, and make humorous comments to keep up a lively group atmosphere. Thus, cooperative learning reinforces the human need for contact and communication with others.

Further, a cooperative rather than a competitive approach in the classroom creates an environment where students feel they can succeed (Deutsch, 1960). Members of cooperative groups are largely oriented toward making a contribution that helps the group accomplish a task where everyone is accountable. There is energy available for the arousal of intrinsic motives such as interest, curiosity, and understanding since the members of the group are not oriented toward outdoing one another. Moreover, cooperative activities reduce the fear of failure and offer more students the chance to feel successful through meeting group goals.

Cooperative learning also builds a classroom climate/environment that includes a variety of perspectives. Such an environment affirms all students because it values their contributions, and it also emphasizes the importance of critical thinking by examining topics from different viewpoints. This is why many, if not most, teachers committed to cooperative learning deliberately create heterogeneous groups.

Ambrose, et al (2010), within the context of "tone," claim that "course climate is also about how the instructor communicates with students, the level of hospitableness that students perceive, and the more general range of inclusion and comfort that students experience" (p. 176). Cooperative learning facilitates student-faculty communication because it is one-on-one or small-group to teacher. The instructor is not remaining aloof behind a lectern. This hospitable climate is further enhanced by positive student-student interactions within small groups where all students are included and valued as they work together on common tasks.

The group processing aspects of cooperative learning help both faculty and students monitor the classroom environment so that they can take corrective actions, if needed. Fortunately, such corrections are rare because cooperative learning's attention to social and leadership skills empower students with the tools to create a positive climate.

Thus, given all these convergent factors, faculty wanting to motivate their students can feel confident that cooperative learning approaches can positively impact major aspects of motivation, particularly the classroom environment.

References

Ambrose, S. A., Bridges, M. W., DiPietro, M., Lovett, M. C., & Norman, M .K. (2010) *How learning works: Seven research-based principles for smart teaching*. San Francisco, CA: Jossey Bass.

Davidson, N. (1976). Motivation of students in small-group learning of mathematics. *Frostburg State College Journal of Mathematics Education, 11,* 1-18.

Davidson, N., Major, C. H., & Michaelsen, L. (2014). *Journal of Excellence in College Teaching, 25*(3 & 4).

Deutsch, Morton, (1960). The effects of cooperation and competition upon group process. In *Group Dynamics: Research and Theory*, pp. 414-448. Edited by D. Cartwright and A. Zander, 2nd ed. New York, NY: Harper and Row.

Millis, B. J. (Ed). (2010). *Cooperative learning in higher education: Across the disciplines, across the academy*. Sterling, VA: Stylus.

Millis, B. J. & Cottell, P. G. (1998). *Cooperative learning for higher education faculty*. American Council on Education, Oryx Press [Later available through Greenwood Press, now out-of-print].

Svinicki, M. D. (2016). Motivation: An Updated Analysis. IDEA Paper No. 59. Manhattan, KS: The IDEA Center. Retrieved January 6, 2018, from https://www.ideaedu.org/Portals/0/Uploads/Documents/IDEA%20Papers/IDEA%20Papers/PaperIDEA_59.pdf

Barbara Millis, retired
Neil Davidson, University of Maryland

Helping Introverts Thrive During Cooperative Group Work

High Impact Practice: Collaborative Assignments and Projects

A review of over two dozen books on college teaching—including such "best-sellers" as Davis' (2009) *Tools for Teaching*, Fink's (2015) *Creating Significant Learning Experiences*, and Nilson's (2010) *How People Learn*—turned up no references to introversion or extroversion. These omissions are surprising given the wide acceptance of Carl Jung's personality classifications. Virtually everyone is aware of these distinctions and knows that introverts prefer small groups rather than large group gatherings. After time with people, introverts need time alone to re-charge (Myers, 1980, 1995). Most people have formed judgments about their own classification. "I hate parties!" claim people who regard themselves as introverts. "Let me read a book or play video games by myself." Self-classified introverted students are as likely to declare: "I hate group work! Let me work alone."

Charges about the detrimental effects of group work on introverts have been bolstered by the publication of Cain's (2012) book, *Quiet,* and her subsequent presentations such as her 2012 TED talk "The Power of Introverts." In the latter, she emphatically implores the audience to, "Stop the madness for constant group work. Just stop it." Unfortunately, this exhortation, focused on our workplaces and schools, rests on allegations about detrimental effects such as "groupthink" that ignore the type of group work involved. All group work is NOT created equal.

Advocates of highly structured group work, such as cooperative learning, are careful to identify the elements that set it apart from looser forms of group work. Most researcher agree on these characteristics articulated by Davidson (1994, 2002) and Davidson, Major, & Michaelsen (2014): Task or learning activity suitable for groups; small group interaction focused on the task; cooperation and mutual helpfulness; interdependence (positive interdependence), meaning that students have vested reasons to work together; and individual accountability and responsibility, meaning that students earn the grades or other rewards they receive. Millis (2010) and others would add two more characteristics to this list: group processing (both students and faculty members pay attention to what transpires in the groups) and the deliberate development of social and leadership skills. Although not a "given," many cooperative learning practitioners also purposefully create diverse groups.

Under these highly structured conditions, introverts, as a matter of fact, can thrive. The research base for the efficacy of cooperative learning is long-standing and robust. Researchers such as Johnson, Johnson and Smith (2006) have noted the following positive effects: student achievement, higher order thinking skills, self esteem and self confidence as learners, intergroup relations, friendships across racial and ethnic boundaries, interpersonal skills, social acceptance, and the ability to take the perspective of another person. These studies occurred without taking into account differences between introverts or extroverts; thus, the results apply to all students. Such outcomes could not have occurred had group work negatively impacted introverts, who make up a sizable proportion of the population, ranging from 33% to 40% depending on whom you consult.

Further, advocates of cooperative learning employ practices that even skeptics such as Susan Cain agree benefit introverts. Cooperative learning groups are deliberately small, typically no larger than four, and are often composed of three (as recommended by the Johnsons) and two (pair work is common). Think-Pair-Share (Lyman, 1992), for example, is probably the best-known cooperative learning approach. During this procedure, instructors build in "wait time," wherein students either reflect or write before turning to a single partner, a comfortable scenario for introverts, who typically abhor "small talk" but welcome in-depth discussions with one other person. In pairs, each student interviews the other for the same designated time. The final small-group or whole-class "share" portion of the procedure is nonthreatening because introverts may remain silent or may choose to speak after having experienced rehearsal time and feedback with their partner. As noted earlier, cooperative learning requires "positive interdependence," often using approaches that encourage equal participation and discourage dominance. For example, during a Three-step Interview (Kagan & Kagan, 2009), students interview each other in low-risk pairs, each student having the same amount of time to respond. When two pairs unite to form a team of four, the individual members introduce their partners, not themselves, in the same amount of time. The structured nature of Think-Pair-Share and the Three-step Interview ensures that introverted voices are heard. Almost twenty years ago, James Cooper (1990) noted a hallmark of cooperative learning as "Structure! Structure! Structure!" Introverts, as many experts attest, greatly prefer structured, predictable activities to chaotic surprises.

In her TED talk Susan Cain disparages unstructured group work, wherein participants are often swayed by dominant, charismatic talkers whose ideas may be worthless. She boldly announces: "Much better for everybody to go off by themselves, generate their own ideas freed from the distortions of group dynamics, and then come together as a team to talk them through in a well-managed environment . . .." Ironically, Cain is describing exactly what occurs in cooperative learning practices predicated on deep learning. Rhem (1995) and McKay and Kember (1997) describe the four characteristics of deep learning as follows: (1) An in-depth, well-structured knowledge base focused on concepts, not mere facts; (2) An emphasis on intrinsic motivation; (3) Active learning; and, (4) Interaction with others, including the teacher and other students. Millis and Cottell (1998) and Millis (2002, 2010) recommend a structured sequence based on these deep learning principles, wherein students complete on their own motivating pre-class assignments, which are then processed and discussed in face-to-face cooperative groups using active learning and student-student and student-teacher interactions, exactly the procedure that Cain advocates. Interestingly, this is the same sequence used in what is called Flipped Learning, wherein introverts and other students are independently exposed to new concepts in what Talbert (2017) describes as Individual Space and then go deeper into the material in what he calls Group Space.

While introverts dislike unstructured group work, they do well in structured cooperative learning, which provides equal participation, prevents dominances, and allows time to think before speaking. Having taught thousands of introverts using cooperative learning for well over thirty years, the two authors can attest that introverts, like other students, do indeed thrive during cooperative group work.

References

Cain, S. (2012). *Quiet: The Power of introverts in a world where people can't stop talking.* New York, NY: Random House.

Cain, S. (2012, February). The power of introverts. TED Talk. Retrieved November 4, 2017 from https://www.ted.com/talks/susan_cain_the_power_of_introverts

Cooper, J. (1990, May). Cooperative learning and college teaching: Tips from the trenches. *The Teaching Professor*, 4(5), 1-2.

Davidson, N. (1994, 2002). Cooperative and collaborative learning: An integrated perspective. In J. Thousand, R. Villa, & A. Nevin (Eds.), *Creativity and collaborative learning: A practical guide for empowering teachers and students* (pp. 13-30). Baltimore, MD: Brookes.

Davidson, N., Major, C., and Michaelsen, L. (Eds). (2014). Small group learning in higher education – cooperative, collaborative, problem-based and team-based learning. *Journal on Excellence in College Teaching*, 25 (3&4),?.

Davis, B. G. (2009). *Tools for teaching.* (2nd ed.) San Francisco, CA: Jossey-Bass.

Fink, L. D. (2013). *Creating significant learning experiences: An integrated approach to designing college courses.* (2nd ed.) San Francisco, CA: Jossey-Bass.

Johnson, D. W., Johnson, R. T. & Smith, K. A. (2006). *Active learning: Cooperation in the college classroom.* (3rd ed). Edina, MN: Interaction.

Kagan, S. & Kagan, M. (2009). *Kagan cooperative learning.* San Clemente, CA: Kagan Publishing.

Lyman, F. (1992). Think-pair-share, thiinktrix, thinklinks, and weird facts: An interactive system for cooperative thinking. In Davidson, N. & Worsham, T. (1992). *Enhancing thinking through cooperative learning*. New York, NY: Teachers College Press. 169-181.

McKay, J. & Kember, D. (1997). Spoon feeding leads to regurgitation: A better diet can result in more digestible learning outcomes. *Higher Education Research and Development*, 6(1), 55-67.

Millis, B. J. (2002). Enhancing learning—and more!—Through cooperative learning. IDEA Paper No. 38. Manhattan, KS: The IDEA Center. Retrieved November 4, 2017, from https://www.ideaedu.org/Portals/0/Uploads/Documents/IDEA%20Papers/IDEA%20Papers/IDEA_Paper_38.pdf

Millis, B. J. (2010), Promoting deep learning. IDEA Paper No. 47. Manhattan, KS: The IDEA Center. Retrieved November 4, 2017, from https://www.ideaedu.org/Portals/0/Uploads/Documents/IDEA%20Papers/IDEA%20Papers/IDEA_Paper_47.pdf

Millis, B. J. (Ed). (2010). *Cooperative learning in higher education: Across the disciplines, across the academy*. Sterling, VA: Stylus.

Millis, B. J. & Cottell, P. G. (1998). *Cooperative learning for higher education faculty*. American Council on Education, Oryx Press [Later available through Greenwood Press, now out-of-print].

Myers, I. B. (1980). *Gifts Differing: Understanding Personality Type*. Davies-Black Publishing; Reprint edition (May 1, 1995).

Nilson, L. B. (2016). *Teaching at Its best: A research-based resource for college instructors*. (4th ed). San Francisco: Jossey-Bass.

Rhem, J. (1995). Close-up: Going deep. *The National Teaching & Learning Forum*, 5(1), 4.

Talbert, R. (2017). *Flipped learning: A guide for higher education faculty*. Sterling, VA: Stylus.

Barbara Millis, retired faculty development director and English professor
Neil Davidson, Professor Emeritus, University of Maryland

12 Step Recovery Program for Lectureholics:

Workshop Summary

Since the publication of our article "Twelve Step Recovery Program for Lectureholics" in 1997, we have offered numerous workshops on this topic. The design combines cooperative learning, several high-impact practices, classroom management, and classroom assessment in a recovery framework.

Diagnostic Oral Quiz

Please shout yes or no!
1. Are you irresistibly drawn to the podium every time you enter a classroom?
2. Do you become irritable when a student's raised hand interrupts your monologue?
3. Are members of the class still nameless to you by mid-term?
4. Do you love the sound of your voice?
5. Do you believe that students eagerly await the pearls of wisdom that drop from your lips?
6. Do you believe that students should eagerly await your pearls of wisdom?

If you answered 'yes' to any of these questions, you could be suffering from an addiction common to many college professors: excessive, out of control lecturing. But don't despair! We were once lectureholics ourselves, and know that full recovery is possible. This is a 12 step recovery program designed especially for lectureholics--those addicted to continuous non-stop lecturing.

We have enormous respect for the Alcoholics Anonymous program, which has helped countless individuals. In our recovery program for lectureholics, we have adapted and condensed the twelve-step program of Alcoholics Anonymous and Overeaters Anonymous.

Overview of the Key Steps of the Recovery Program

Because of some redundancy among the steps, we have condensed the twelve-step program into six key steps. This procedure provides an accelerated cure!
1. Admit that you have a problem with your lecturing.
2. Turn yourself over to an educational power greater than yourself.
3. Make a searching and fearless inventory of your teaching practices.
4. Atone for your "wrongs."
5. Maintain the improvements you have made in your teaching practices.
6. Spread the word to other lecture addicts.

Step One: Admit You Have a Problem with Your Lecturing

The first step of recovery is admitting that you have a problem with your lecturing. Step One involves two activities: sharing Rock-Bottom (Lectureholic) Stories, and identifying the Tell-Tale Signs of a Lectureholic.

Rock-Bottom Stories

Procedure: Two-Step Interview (Kagan)

Within each pair, each person is given a time limit of perhaps 60 seconds to share.
1. Tell your story to your partner; partner listens.
2. Partner tells you his or her story; you listen.
3. Whole-class sharing of a few stories by the people who experienced them.

Partners take turns sharing their worst lecture stories: Describe a "rock-bottom" lecture (either your own or one you witnessed). What made it so awful?
Then, a few stories are shared with the whole group.

Tell-Tale Signs of a Lectureholic

To determine the nature of the problem of lecturing, participants brainstorm the tell-tale signs of a lectureholic.

4-S Brainstorming (Kagan)

Designate a group recorder.
Record ideas using the 4 S's.
Speed: Let's get as many ideas as fast as we can.
Support: All ideas are accepted when stated.
Silly: Let's get more silly ideas and be creative.
Synergy: Build on the ideas of others.
Set a time limit.

In brainstorming, "silly" ideas can be creative, imaginative, wild, etc,. To maximize creativity, no criticism is permitted when ideas are being generated. After the time elapses, evaluation of ideas occurs.

Procedure: The Round-Robin Reporter Line-up (Davidson and Solomon, 1997)

Reporters from each group line up in front of the class and take turns speaking. In round-robin fashion, each reporter shares one tell-tale sign (lectureholics will try to dominate by sharing many signs). Continue with round-robin until all ideas are shared with class.

This is a good alternative to having each group present its full report, one group after another, which can be quite boring.

Step 2: Admit that there is an educational power (or perspective) greater than yourself, and turn yourself over to that higher power or perspective.

Lecturette: In all the 12 Step Programs, participants choose a higher power as they personally perceive it. In our program, we are suggesting an additional higher power relevant for educators—the Higher Power of Active Learning.

What is active learning? Active learning may involve...
- learning by doing.
- discussing with others.
- thinking, reasoning, problem-solving, etc.
- reading, writing, drawing, computing, doing kinesthetic activities, making music, etc.
- Active learning is not simply listening.

Discussion Question: What are some successful ways to employ active learning in the classroom?

<u>Procedure: Numbered Heads Together (Kagan)</u>

Each group member receives a number from 1 to 4.
Group discussion
Prepare to respond
Person who reports out for the group will be identified by the number
Sample active learning strategies suggested by participants include: peer teaching, peer editing, simulations, creating graphic organizers, group problem-solving.

Step 3: Make a searching and fearless inventory of your teaching practices.

In traditional 12 Step programs, this step is described as a searching and fearless "moral" inventory. For our program, we see this as an educational rather than a moral issue.

Lecturette: The Emperor's New Clothes

Just like the Emperor in the fairytale, teachers may not see themselves as their students see them. We don't want to delude ourselves. We should engage in frequent reality checks by gathering data to help us see ourselves through our students' eyes.

Approaches to taking inventory
- Student evaluations
- Peer observations

- Video-taping
- Suggestion box
- Focus groups at midterm or earlier (i.e. Another instructor comes into your class to solicit feedback from students about what is going well and what needs to be changed.)

Comments: Student evaluations are good for long-term growth of instructors; however, by the time we get the results, students are long gone. Therefore, receiving student feedback throughout the semester can provide valuable reality checks which leads to improved teaching.

Classroom assessment tools:
- One-minute paper (Angelo and Cross)
- Visual comprehension signals (using hands)
- Diagnostic quiz
- Listening in on group discussions
- Attending to group feedback

<u>Attending to group feedback:</u> The teacher invites students to share informal and formal observations about the lesson or group interaction.
Others…

Discussion Questions:
Among the approaches to taking inventory of your teaching, which ones would you use in your own classes?
Which approaches have you already used and how well did they work?
Before discussion using think-pair-share, we invite participants to add other successful approaches to the list of assessment tools.

Procedure: Think-Pair-Share (Lyman)

- Teacher poses to the class a question for discussion.
- Students silently think about the question posed.
- Students discuss question with their partner.
- Students share responses with the whole class.

Step 4: Atone for your "wrongs."
After taking your fearless inventory, you may be devastated with GUILT about your past teaching. However, obsessing about your guilt will only make matters worse

and will not improve your teaching. We suggest that you be action-oriented, not guilt-oriented.

Lecturette: Ways to Atone by Changing your Practice
- Enroll in workshops for faculty.
- Read about active learning (AL) strategies.
- Try a new AL strategy with your students.
- Observe another teacher using AL.
- Form an AL support group.
- Conduct action research on the effects of AL on student achievement, attitudes and attendance.
- Read your students' evaluations with an open mind and try some of their suggestions.

Ways to Atone by Doing Penance

- Invite former students to lecture to you!
- Attend boring, endless lectures and sit in a hard chair. .
- Purge yellowed lecture notes from your files.
- Be present during your office hours to respond to "stupid questions".
- Force yourself to volunteer at remedial learning centers.
- Find alternate explanations for difficult ideas.
- Videotape the faces of our students as we lecture, and watch these in slow motion.

Step 5: Maintain the improvements you have made in your teaching.

Lecturette: For any recovering addict, staying on the wagon is a challenging aspect of recovery. Recovering lectureholics must be sensitive to triggers that propel them into non-stop lecturing. Internal triggers include vocal exercises before class to warm up your voice, gargling, and having fantasies about receiving a standing ovation. Environmental triggers include lecture halls with imposing podiums for your copious notes, spotlights and theatre style seating.

Therefore, our recommendations are:
- Be aware of internal and environmental cues that trigger your addiction
- Remember to meditate or reflect on your teaching, especially right after class.
- When faced with temptation to lecture,

- Call your sponsor or support team.

Discussion Question:
What are some other affirmations that might work well for you?

Procedure: Formulate-Share-Listen-Create (Johnsons)

- Formulate an affirmation of your own.
- Share the affirmation with your team.
- Listen to others' ideas.
- Create a new affirmation as a team.

Teams share their affirmations with the whole group. The sharing could take many forms such as round-robin line-up, group reports to the whole class, or a gallery walk (affirmations posted on chart paper).

Step 6: Spread the word to other addicts.
- Here are some recommendations for spreading the word about active learning:
- Model the techniques of active learning
- Embody this higher power in your teaching
- Meet regularly with your sponsor or support group
- Share ideas and resources for active learning
- Emphasize interactive lecturing by alternating short lectures with brief pair or group activities
- Call the Lectureholics hotline: 1-800-LECTURE.

References

Angelo, T. and Cross, P. K. (1993). *Classroom assessment techniques* (2nd ed.). San Francisco, CA: Jossey-Bass.

Alcoholics Anonymous big book. (2001). (4th ed.). AA World Services. New York, NY.

Bonwell, C. C., and Eison, J. A. 1991. *Active learning: Creating excitement in the classroom.* Washington, D.C.: ASHE-ERIC.

Bowman, S. (2003). *Preventing death by lecture: Terrific tips for turning listeners into learners.* Glenbrook, NV: Beauperson Publishing Co.

Davidson, N. & Worsham, T. (1992). *Enhancing thinking through cooperative learning.* New York, NY: Teachers College Press.

Dunn, J. P. (1994). Reflections of a recovering lectureholic. *Forum,* 3(6), 1-3.

Jensen, E. and Davidson, N. (1997). Twelve step recovery program for lectureholics. *College Teaching*, 45(3), 102-103.

Johnson, D. W., Johnson, R. T. & Smith, K.A. (2006). *Active learning: Cooperation in the college classroom*. Edina, MN: Interaction Book Company.

Kagan, S. & Kagan, M. (2009). *Kagan cooperative learning*. San Clemente, CA: Kagan Publishing.

Lyman, F. (1992). Think-pair-share, thiinktrix, thinklinks, and weird facts: An interactive system for cooperative thinking. In Davidson, N. & Worsham, T. (1992). 169-181

Neil Davidson, University of Maryland
Emily B. Jensen, Harford Community College
Richard D. Solomon, University of Maryland

Learning the Agile Way with Iterative and Incremental Projects

I have developed a pedagogic framework that uses iterative and incremental student projects to motivate learning and achievement. This framework is aligned with constructionism, which observes that students learn by making and sharing artifacts (Papert & Harel, 1991) and studio-based learning courses, which see artifact-creation as the manifestation of student learning (Hundhausen, Narayanan, & Crosby, 2008). These academic theories are combined with the philosophy of agile software development (Beck *et al.*, 2001), particularly the values of iterative and incremental development. Combining these leads to an approach in which students are continuously engaged in feedback loops of planning, execution, evaluation, and reflection renders great benefits.

The framework is defined by the following characteristics:
- *Collaborative.* Students work in teams to create something larger than an individual could accomplish.
- *Community-Connected.* Student teams develop projects with or for a community partner.
- *Iterative.* Students plan work for fixed timeboxes. For example, a team commits to addressing particular needs during a three-week iteration, and during that time, the team holds itself accountable to those goals.

- *Incremental.* Each iteration produces artifacts that can be evaluated by, and have potential benefit to, the community partner. This approach is in contrast to conventional planning approaches in which legitimate value is manifest only upon integration late in the project; with an incremental approach, value can be delivered to the partner every one to four weeks.
- *Reflective.* Each iteration concludes with both collective and individual reflections. Students' written reflections are evaluated for their structure as well as their content, so that each iteration improves the precision of both their writing and their thinking.

This framework can be applied in any context where project-based learning is appropriate and a community partner can be involved. The following three examples are taken from three courses for different audiences, and these illustrate how the framework is adaptable to different circumstances.

The first example is a project-oriented course for Computer Science majors and minors. The course comes after the first two foundational programming courses, and it introduces students to professional tools and techniques. Nine weeks of the course are devoted to a major project that is completed in three three-week iterations. Teams of three or four students collaboratively identify a target audience and a problem that can be solved through software. Teams articulate work items as user stories (Cohn, 2004) and prioritize these stories into a product backlog as in Scrum (Schwaber & Sutherland, 2017). During the iteration planning meeting, they commit to a high-priority subset of stories to implement as software features. Teams are required to test each increment with representative end users as part of the iteration. At the end of each iteration, I guide the teams in collective retrospectives (Kerth, 2001; Kua, 2013), and each student completes an individual essay that aligns their personal experiences with the course's essential questions (McTighe & Wiggins, 2013).

The second example is a course on serious game design. The students spend half of the semester designing an original educational game for a local non-profit organization such as a museum or school. These are primarily analog games such as board games or card games, although students with a technical bent may produce digital games. Students complete an iteration each week, producing successively-refined prototypes during the semester. In-class presentations allow the students to share what design questions they addressed and how they evaluated their prototype. The final exam consists of reflective essays about the artifacts and processes of the course.

The third example is a multidisciplinary game production studio I lead, in which approximately ten upper-division undergraduates from different backgrounds work together to produce an original educational video game. We deploy user story mapping

(Patton, 2014) to manage the project. Team retrospective meetings held after each two-week iteration authorize the team to modify their methodology. Additionally, students submit intermediate work products (Cockburn, 2006) into a digital portfolio and write essays on how these products facilitated reflective practice.

My framework combines academic rigor with industrial best-practices. It manifests most of the eight key elements of high-impact educational practices—high performance expectations, significant investment by students over extended time, substantive interactions with faculty and peers, frequent feedback, periodic reflection, and real-world applications—and some instantiations have featured all eight (Kuh & O'Donnell, 2013). The iterative and incremental approach combats the tendency students have toward procrastination, and it manifests the agile philosophy that every action should add value to the customer. The students are engaged in rigorous writing activity appropriate to their discourse community (Swales 1990). Once students understand an increment as a *potentially shippable product* rather than a simple milestone, they come to recognize the critical value of sustained effort: no room to be lackadaisical exists when there is a limited timebox to design, develop, evaluate, and present tangible progress. The collective and individual retrospectives are valuable as both learning experiences and assessment instruments (Gestwicki, 2016). As service-learning experiences, the courses can provide tangible benefits to community partners. Finally, I will note that these courses tend to be fun for me to teach: every project is different and explores new territory, and so I can learn with the students as I mentor them through the process.

References

Beck, K., Beedle, M., van Bennekum, A., Cockburn, A., Cunningham, W., Fowler, M, Grenning, J., Highsmith, J., & Thomas, D. (2001). *Manifesto for Agile Software Development*. AgileManifesto.org.

Cockburn, A. (2006). *Agile Software Development: The Cooperative Game*. Addison-Wesley.

Cohn, M. (2004). *User Stories Applied*. Addison-Wesley Professional.

Gestwicki, P. (2016). "Using periodic retrospective assessment in multidisciplinary project teams." In Blythe, H., Sweet, C., & Carpenter, R. (Eds.), *It works for me, metacognitively*, (pp. 160-2). Stillwater, OK: New Forums Press.

Hundhausen, C. D., Narayanan, N. H., & Crosby, M. E. (2008). "Exploring studio-based instructional models for computing education." In *Proceedings of the 39th SIGCSE Technical Symposium on Computer science education* (SIGCSE '08), pp392-6. ACM.

Kerth, N. L. (2001). *Project Retrospectives*. Dorset House.

Kua, P. (2013). *The Retrospective Handbook*. CreateSpace Independent Publishing.

Kuh, G. D. (2008). *High-Impact Educational Practices: What They Are, Who Has Access to Them, and Why They Matter*. AAC&U.

Kuh, G. D. & O'Donnell, K. (2013). *Ensuring Quality & Taking High-Impact Practices to Scale*. AAC&U.

McTighe, J. & Wiggins, G. (2013). *Essential Questions*. Association for Supervision & Curriculum Development.

Papert, S. & Harel, I. (1991). "Situating Constructionism". In Harel, I. & Papert, S. (Eds.), *Constructionism*. Ablex.

Patton, J. (2014). *User Story Mapping*. O'Reilly.

Schwaber, K. & Sutherland, J. (2017). *The Scrum Guide*, November 2017 edition. ScrumGuides.org.

Swales, J. M. (1990). *Genre Analysis: English in Academic and Research Settings*. Cambridge University Press.

Paul Gestwicki, Ball State University

Effective and Interactive Group Assignments in an Online Course

Two years ago I [Teresa] redesigned my Theatre History course from a face to face format to an online class. While the content and assessments translated well to the online environment, I had trouble replicating the kind of interactive group work that I had done in the face to face course. Not surprisingly, the one comment I repeatedly got from students was that they wished the course allowed them more opportunities to interact with each other.

To address this issue, I partnered with our Instructional Designer over mobile technology to find ways to leverage technology to support more collaborative online group projects. The solution we landed on was to use our university's Google suite to provide an online, collaborative space in which the students could work, and then bring their final work back to our LMS.

Based on that approach, I re-designed the course to include 5 group assignments. These assignments occur every two to three weeks. While each assignment is different, in that we are studying different periods of theatre history, they all follow this basic framework:

1. I randomly create groups of 3 students (each time the groups are different).
2. I create a Google folder for each group and make it available for all the students in the group to view and edit.

3. I assign a problem for the group to solve (using what they learned from that week's reading and additional research), and create a Google Doc, with a prompt, for each group to write their answer to the problem.

4. Each student within the group is expected to do research that will support their collective answer. Research assets are shared in the group folder where all members can review and analyze the results.

5. After a collaborative commenting process, students create one final answer. Each group submits their answer to the problem using our LMS discussion board, and each student then must read and respond to two different groups' posts.

For example, in the third week of the course, in which we studied the theatre of Ancient Greece, the students read two plays, *Lysistrata* and *Oedipus Rex*. Each student was responsible for finding a review of a production of each play, looking for reasons the producing company chose that play to perform. Then, as a group, they considered and answered the following question:

> Your group will imagine that you are members of a theatre company that are charged with deciding which play your company will perform next. You must choose which of these two plays you should produce, and then write a statement to your theatre company about the reasons for your choice. Your statement should include one reason based on the research done by your group of other productions of the play, and one reason based on what we learned about why this play was originally performed (from our historical reading during this module).

By using a Google Doc for their collaborative work, my online students can asynchronously post their research and comment on others' work in their own time. Comments stay live within the document, updating regularly, and are automatically shared with members of the group. In this way, the student group can polish their answer collaboratively before submitting the final version to our LMS discussion board.

In addition to creating the collaborative space for students, the Google folders also have additional benefits, including:
- Having students work in a Google Doc allows me to track interactions on their written work, to see who participated in the discussions/editing, and to review what changes they made to their work along the way.
- The shared folder for each group makes it easy for me to grade the assignment, as all pieces are in one place.
- The folders also help me to easily collect artifacts of students' work for overall assessment of student performance in our department.
- Google folders grant students continued access, allowing them to more easily use materials from the course for future portfolios.

Not only were there benefits for me as the instructor in creating these group assignments, but the students found them useful as well. When asked to reflect on which assignments during the semester most helped them achieve one of our Course Learning Outcomes, multiple students referenced the group projects as work that helped them learn in the course. One student wrote, "The group [projects] were helpful in [achieving the Learning Outcome of 'form and defend your own aesthetic judgments orally and in writing'] because I could get feedback on a particular costume or set design and then defend my ideas... I would often get feedback from classmates that really opened my perspective" (I. Berenson, Unit IV exam, 2017).

Teresa Focarile, Boise State University
Lana Grover, Boise State University

The Promise and Challenge of Synchronous Online Cooperative Learning

The current standard paradigm for online learning involves asynchronous learning. We propose to expand that paradigm to include synchronous elements to the general course design, specifically cooperative learning (CL). Cooperative learning in any classroom, traditional or online, must include a synchronous event: all members are present at the same time in the same space. A synchronous form of online CL simulates face-to-face interaction available in a live classroom but conducted through screen-to-screen communication. The inclusion of synchronous components carries the benefit of increased student engagement and community-building, thereby maximizing the potential for student learning and successful completion.

The rationale for synchronous online CL is based on the powerful body of classroom CL research results summarized in Davidson, Major, and Michaelsen (2014). These include academic achievement, higher order thinking skills, interpersonal skills, intergroup relations, and more. We predict that the benefits of CL will transfer from the synchronous classroom environment to the synchronous online environment, but not necessarily to an asynchronous online environment.

Proposed synchronous course components would include meetings of all students enrolled in the course with the instructor. The compatibility of time zones in which global learners operate must be taken into consideration by instructors incorporating synchronous CL into their online courses. Furthermore, in the ideal platform, the professor would share the course material in multimedia formats with all students present; the students and the professor would see and hear one another on the screen, enabled by the use of cameras; and students could be divided into groups to work on tasks or documents as in effective face to face cooperation.

Questions and Challenges

The same questions apply to CL practices in the face-to-face environment and online with the caveat that the faculty have appropriate, effective technology available. Issues include group formation, assessment and evaluation, dominators and non-participators, and leadership (plus time-zone compatibility). Are groups to be self-directed and managed, or will there be some instructor intervention? If multiple groups are online at the same time, will the instructor be checking in on them? Can groups share information with one another, given existing technology?

In classroom CL, there are many procedures such as interview, round-robin and roundtable, think-pair-share, numbered heads together, and jigsaw, to name a few. In the classroom, a group of four can readily split into two pairs for discussion, and then re-combine to share results from the pairs. Is this readily possible in an online environment?

Solutions

In the online classroom, a degree of creativity and flexibility of instructors provide some solutions. For example, in peer editing of one another's papers, the drafts can be submitted by email for critique. Feedback can be given individually by email or in an online seminar class or both. However, those options resemble unstructured group work or collaborative learning, not cooperative learning per se. Faculty can also utilize a combination of synchronous and asynchronous online elements, depending on the goal of the activities in development.

Now let's consider the technology available for synchronous online CL. The video conference technology for synchronous online learning is improving rapidly, as did the technology for audio conference calls. One of the technologies available now is the Adobe Connect platform. Adobe Connect is an online video conferencing and presentation platform. It allows the participants to hear and see one another. Additionally, the presenter(s) can upload documents, share a computer screen, play videos to the whole group, and draw on a whiteboard in a live classroom. The host can designate presenters as desired. Meetings can be recorded and edited, and the archives are easily shared distributing a URL.

For example, Brescia University has used Adobe Connect since Summer 2014 in its online program, which requires students to attend a one-hour per week, mandatory live chat session. In these joint, synchronous sessions with all students and the professor, instructors can lecture, facilitate group discussions, or engage in active learning exercises of various types, depending on their personal teaching methodology. At the professor's discretion, students can be given video and microphone rights, which allows them to be seen and heard in the classroom.

Based on experiences with hosting weekly class chat with students and online pedagogy sessions with faculty, Adobe Connect offers great promise for cooperative learning in the online classroom. Webex or other platforms that offer similar features and reliability could facilitate comparable interactions. Cooperative learning can be managed through these rooms with the use of break-out chats within the room for pairs or small groups. In these break-outs, if students are given microphone rights by the instructor, they can speak with one another, and with video rights enabled, they can see one another as well. Students can also be given presenter rights within these groups to enable the sharing of documents.

Another technological feature enabling student cooperation and learning is the availability of private chats with one another at the instructor's discretion. This feature can allow for activities such as think-pair-share very easily. Like new learning strategies in classrooms, students will likely take some time to adjust; however, the potential benefits of cooperative learning strategies in online classrooms are tremendous. If instructors and students approach these technologies with an open mind and adapt successfully to cooperative learning in an online, synchronous environment, we could see benefits in learning and skill development, as well as in retention and graduation rates.

Platforms such as Adobe Connect or Webex are already used for collaborative faculty communities, for building online student communities, with a brave few using it precisely for cooperative learning activities. With the ever-growing body of evidence showing the effectiveness of active-engagement methodologies for student attainment of knowledge and skills, the academic community at large has a tremendous amount to gain from openly embracing the synchronous elements of online education and cooperative learning online. Since the needed technology has come to fruition, the promise of synchronous online CL can now be realized.

References

Angelino, L. M., Williams, F. K. & Vatvig, D. (2007). Strategies to engage online students and reduce attrition rates, *Journal of Educators Online, 4*(2).

Barcelona, R. J., & Rockey, D. L. (2010). Using collaborative learning technologies to facilitate effective group work, *Journal of Physical Education, Recreation & Dance, 81*(4), 12-15.

Berge, Z. L. (1995). Facilitating computer conferencing: Recommendations from the Field, *Educational Technology, 35*(1), 22.

Bonham, S. (2011). Whole class laboratories with google docs, *Physics Teacher, 49*(1), 22-23.

Casanova, M., & Ibis, M. A. (2012). Online cooperative learning and key interpsychological mechanisms: An exploratory study through the analysis of the discourse content, *Creative Education, 3*(8), 1345-1353.

Cheng, K. W. K. (2009). The effect of web-based collaborative learning methods to the accountant courses in technical education, *College Student Journal, 43*(3), 755-765.

Davidson, N., Major, C., & Michaelsen, L. (Eds) (2014). Small group learning in higher education: Co-operative, collaborative, problem based, and team based learning, *Journal on Excellence in College Teaching, 25*(3, 4).

Dixon, M. D. (2010). Creating effective student engagement in online courses: What do students find engaging, *Journal of the Scholarship of Teaching and Learning, 10*(2), 1-13.

Denton, D. W. (2012). Enhancing instruction through constructivism, cooperative learning, and cloud computing, *TechTrends, 56*(4), 34-41.

Futch, L. (2000). Cooperative learning in online courses. Unpublished Paper. http://pegasus.cc.ucf.edu/~l-futch/cooperative.pdf (retrieved June. 2014)

Hutchinson, D. (2007). Teaching practices for effective cooperative learning in an online learning environment (OLE). *Journal of Information Systems Education, 18*(3), 357-367.

Ku, H. Y., Tseng, H. W., & Akarasriworn, C. (2013). Collaboration factors, teamwork satisfaction, and student attitudes toward online collaborative learning, *Computers in Human Behavior, 29*(3), 922-929.

Lo, H. C. (2013). Design of online report writing based on constructive and cooperative learning for a course on traditional general physics experiments, *Journal of Educational Technology & Society, 16*(1), 380-n/a.

McBrien, J. L; Cheng, R.; & Jones, P. (2009). Virtual spaces: Employing a synchronous online classroom to facilitate student engagement in online learning, *The International Review of Research in Open and Distributed Learning, 10*(3).

Ozkan, H. H. (2010). Cooperative learning technique through internet based education: A model proposal, *Education, 130*(3), 499-508.

Young, S. & Bruce, M. A. (2011). Classroom community and student engagement in online Courses, *Journal of Online Learning and Teaching, 7*(2), 219.

Neil Davidson, University of Maryland
Anna Kuthy, Brescia University
Daniel Kuthy, Brescia University
Richard Solomon, University of Maryland

Using Oral History for Collaborative Projects

Oral histories are beneficial not only for history classrooms, but they are invaluable primary sources that help enhance students' understanding of the historical period for any academic discipline. Two pedagogical approaches to using oral history in teaching are passive oral history and active oral history. Passive oral history uses audio or video recordings, transcripts, websites, and other media to connect the student with content for the curricular area of study. Active oral history focuses on the instruction of methodology and prepares students to be researchers to collect their own oral histories (Lanman & Wendling, 2006).

The incorporation of oral history into any assignment or project is a high-impact practice that promotes collaborative learning and structures opportunities to reflect on student-created, rich insights. Under the collaborative learning paradigm, two key goals are learning to work and solve problems with peers, and sharpening one's own understanding by listening seriously to the insights of others, especially those with different backgrounds and life experiences. Approaches range from study groups within a course, to team-based assignments and writing, to cooperative projects and research. Using examples from my course, Reporting for Print Media (renamed In-depth Reporting beginning in spring 2018), I want to highlight the application of oral histories as a collaborative way for educators and students to meet various elements of high-impact practices.

The body of scholarship within the oral history literature is extensive on how to incorporate oral histories into teaching and specific disciplines (Ritchie, 2003; Lanman & Wendling, 2006; Foster, 2013; Tobbell, 2016). This teaching tip shares how oral histories can be incorporated into any course. Oral histories were taught in Reporting for Print Media for fall 2017, with the practice scheduled in the same course for spring 2018. Students were required to complete a passive oral history assignment before conducting active oral history interviews for a semester-long class news project that focused on public education in Kentucky in the years before standardized testing became the norm. For the active oral history component, the students presented their work at the University's Fall Scholars Week in November. Students in the spring course will be required to do the same at the University's Spring Scholars Week in April.

1. Passive Oral History

After weeklong instruction focusing on oral history as an information-gathering technique in journalism, students completed a writing assignment that focused on passive oral history. The objectives of the assignment were to critique an oral history interview based on the material covered (e.g., interviewer talked too much, background noise created distractions) in the lectures and to identify best practices in conducting oral history interviews.

Students accessed their choice of an oral history audio file in the Education and Desegregation collection on the University library's website. Each student listened to an oral history recording and completed a Canvas discussion thread that provided a synopsis of the topics discussed in the interview and a critical analysis. This assignment allowed students to reflect on how to prepare and conduct oral histories, which would become crucial for the active oral history project.

2. Active Oral History

Active oral histories served as the main information-gathering technique for the class news project that concentrated on public education in Kentucky in the years before the stronghold of standardized testing. Students were placed in groups of four to five and assigned an individual who was recruited by the instructor to serve as an oral history subject. Basic information, such as their years of schooling in a K-12 public education system, was provided to each group, which then used the information to research educational issues and topics relevant to the subject's class years and plan questions to ask in the interview. The instructor reviewed the questions and gave feedback on how they could be strengthened.

All interviews were conducted in class using Tascam audio recording equipment purchased with a grant. Any device, such as a smartphone app, would work effectively. However, because the files also would serve as a public resource, quality recordings were necessary. Two of the subjects were able to come to the classroom for the interviews. A third individual conducted the interview via Zoom web conferencing.

Each student in the group played a role. One served as the official interviewer, who could be heard on the audio recording. Another student in the group was designated to tweet during the oral history to provide immediate updates on the project. The project hashtag was #edoralhistory. Other students also tweeted, took photos, or wrote follow-up questions for the interviewer to ask. Each interview lasted approximately 25 to 30 minutes, which was the desired length.

After each interview, the group collaborated to decide which news stories to write, so that various angles could be reported. Every student in the class had to write a news story based on the interview, but the group assigned to the individual subject was required to plan coverage on different aspects of the interview. Audio recordings, stories, photos, and other elements to document the interviews were housed on the project's website, kyeducationstories.omeka.net/. This site will continue to be used for the spring 2018 semester.

Conclusion

By the instructor's incorporating oral histories into class lessons and collaborative projects, students can study issues of today by placing people back into history. Through oral histories, students can understand not only what happened in the past but also how those narrating the past interpreted events and issues. Plus, oral histories offer an opportunity for educators and students to give a voice to those who have not been heard or regarded on issues or topics. For this collaborative project, oral histories proved to be a structured, high-impact practice because it afforded students an opportunity to invest significant time and effort on a topic over an extended period of time and to interact with diverse individuals. Students also have visible outcomes, the website and Scholars Week presentations, to include in their portfolios and demonstrate competency. In essence, oral histories helped to bring learning to life for students.

References

Foster, R. (2013). A storytelling training ground: Oral history in the journalism classroom. Accessed online at https://mospace.umsystem.edu/xmlui/bitstream/handle/10355/41121/analysis.pdf?sequence=2.

Lanman, B. A., & Wendling, L. M. (2006). Introduction in *Preparing the Next Generation of Oral Historians: An Anthology of Oral History Education*, ed. Lanman and Wendling (New York: AltaMira): xix.

Ritchie, D. A. (2003). Teaching oral history, in *Doing Oral History: A Practical Guide*, 2nd ed. (Oxford: Oxford University Press): 188-221.

Tobbell, D. A. (2016). Teaching with oral histories. *Bulletin of the History of Medicine*, 90(1): 128-135. Doi: https://doi.org/10.1353/bhm.2016.0003.

Melony Shemberger, Murray State University

Five Approaches to Implement End-of-Course Group Projects

In the business world, employee work often involves learning in group settings to create a finished task (Editorial Board, 2012). Learning to work as a member of a team is a key skill required when hiring a university graduate (Burke, 2011). Because of the importance of helping students learn about the role of teamwork, I utilize end-of-course group projects to assess key learning objectives ("Why Work," n.d). In this essay, I will discuss five key approaches to effectively implement end-of-course group projects for the classroom.

First, the instructor must thoroughly review with students all requirements for the end-of-course group project (Working In Groups, n.d.). I discuss written syllabus expectations verbally with students three times during the course. These three key points for discussion occur at the beginning, middle, and at the end of the course. This repetition greatly minimizes any future type of student/teacher conflict of what the requirements were for correct completion of the assignment.

Second, setting up the number of students for any group project is an important consideration. I generally allow my students to form a maximum of up to a five-member size for an end-of-course group project. Keeping the group size smaller encourages members to more easily resolve conflict and also helps minimize instances of one member not contributing a fair share of work (Burk, 2011).

Third, I allow my students to form their own groups. I have learned many students prefer to work only with particular members of their class. I usually require students to form their groups no later than the middle of a 15 week semester. This time frame allows students ample time during the semester to get to know other members of their class before they choose to form their group.

During the middle of the semester, I provide students 15-20 minutes of class time to exchange required contact information with each other such as a preferred communication method (phone calls, texts, email) and a preferred document sharing process (Google Docs, Box, etc.,). Requiring students to form a group of their choice no later than the middle of the semester motivates them to begin planning out effective time frames for completing the assignment on time.

Fourth, after forming a group, occasionally students will approach me and attempt to get me involved in resolving different types of conflicts that may occur. My response is always to require students to resolve their group conflicts on their own. My reason for this approach is that in the real business world, group projects will be common and learning to work together as a team to resolve conflict is a key work skill.

Finally, I require a minimum of a 20-30 minute oral presentation based on the end-of-course group project that must involve equal participation by all members. This presentation format provides them with experience of how to orally present results of a group project to others.

In conclusion, I believe that the five approaches discussed in this essay for implementing end-of-course group projects help prepare my students to be more effective team members in their future business career.

References

Anonymous. Why work in groups? (n.d.). University of Birmingham. Retrieved from https:///www.birmingham.ac.uk/schools/metallurge-mataerials/about/cases/group-work/why.aspx

Burke, A. (2011). Group work: How to use groups effectively. *The Journal of Effective Teaching*, II(2), 87-95.

Editorial Board. (2012) The benefits of group projects. *Stanford Daily*. Retrieved from https://www.stanforddaily.com/2012/05/16/editorial-the-benefits-of-group-projects/

Harmon, J. (2014) Don't dismiss the benefits of group projects. Retrieved from http://blog.online.colostate.edu/blog/online-teaching/dont-dismiss-the-benefits-of-group-projects/

Weimer, M. (2013). Five things students can learn through group work. Retrieved from https://www.facultyfocus.com/articles/teaching-professor-blog/five-things-students-can-learn-through-group-work/

Breck A. Harris, Fresno Pacific University

Creating Collaborative Learning with Storytelling

Simmons (2002, p. 11) defines a story as a "narrative account of an event or events – true or fictional." Storytelling, also known by the term personal narrative, is common to people of all cultures and helps us make meaning of our life (Bridge Interactive, 2002). Storytelling helps us to learn from others' experiences and celebrate the victory of others (Bridge Interactive, 2002). If we are wise, stories can also help us to learn from the mistakes of others. According to Maguire (1998), benefits of storytelling include investing our lives with more meaning, connecting us more vitally with others, developing our creativity, strengthening our sense of humor, increasing our courage and confidence, and rendering our lives to be more memorable. Discussing our stories with others helps us internalize and integrate our learning into our conceptual framework of knowledge (Brown, Denning, Groh & Prusak, 2005).

Telling stories in the classroom offers many benefits for both teachers and students. Use of authentic and truthful personal stories by a teacher can be a very powerful way of creating effective communication and collaborative learning with students. In this essay, I will discuss two oral approaches using personal storytelling I utilize in a college-level Business Ethics class.

A key learning outcome in this class is to help students develop their own personal code of ethics and to discover how they will choose to act in different business situations involving ethical choice between right or wrong. In this class, I share my ethical work experiences with students.

One collaborative learning approach I use is to verbally communicate a truthful story with them about one of my prior work experiences –but I share my narrative story with students only to the point where I was required to make an ethical decision of what I considered right or wrong. I then have students form small groups of 3-4 and, based on my personal story, allow them approx. 10 minutes to come to consensus of how their group would decide to act. These small groups are later asked to briefly share their reasons for their ethical decision with all members of the class. After all the groups have reported, I end the exercise by sharing how I chose to act in that ethical situation. I often pass out to students collaborating written documentation to further support the truth of my personal story.

A second collaborative learning storytelling approach is that I create a one- page written summary of an ethical story. Students are asked to read this one-page handout. Students are formed into small groups of 3-4 in. I give the groups ten minutes of time to discuss the story and come to consensus of what they would do. Each student group is then asked to share reasons for their ethical decision with all members of the class. However, after this process, I share a "surprise" with them. The "surprise" I disclose is that the actual subject of the ethical story was myself. This ethical story required me to make a decision of what I considered was right or wrong. I often pass out to students collaborating documents that further support the truth of my personal story.

Simmons (2002) claims that good stories always contain some type of truth and that the storyteller needs to learn to "let go" and tell a genuine story that touches the listener's humanity (p.31). For teachers, personal stories, otherwise known as personal narrative, can be a very effective communication approach to create collaborative learning with students. However, it is critical that these stories be truthful so that you are perceived as being authentic and real by your listeners (Brown, et. al. 2005). I have found that sharing my personal work stories to be a powerful way to build authenticity and connection with students. This process often leads to transformative learning by students about ethical decision-making.

References

Bridge Interactive. (2002). *What do we know about stories?* Retrieved from http://www.bizstorytellers.org/Ia_Storytelling.htm

Brown, J.S., Denning, S., Groh, K. & Prusak, L. (2005). *Storytelling in organizations. Why storytelling is transforming 21st century organizations and management.* Burlington, MA: Elsevier Butterworth-Heinemann.

Maguire, J. (1998). *The power of personal storytelling: Spinning tales to connect with others.* New York: Tarcher/Putnam.

Simmons, A. (2002). *The story factor: Secrets of influence from the art of storytelling.* Cambridge, MS: Perseus Publishing.

Breck A. Harris, Fresno Pacific University

Collaborative Lesson Planning: It Works For Me!

Our university offers a Bachelor of Science degree in Middle Grades Education preparing prospective teachers (PTs) to teach grades 6-9. The PTs are required to choose two concentrations from language arts, social studies, science, and mathematics. PTs choosing mathematics as one of their concentrations must take the course "Teaching Mathematics in the Middle School." Research has shown that the teaching of mathematics should not focus entirely on the content, but should also consider the interactions that occur between teachers, students, and content (Cohen & Ball, 1999). These interactions set the stage for productive mathematical thinking and learning, as well as exposing mathematical misconceptions. In this course, PTs are provided with opportunities to work with peers, through collaborating in a variety of activities and reflecting on their participation, in the hope that it will initiate collaboration amongst their students and with their colleagues across their future careers.

Collaborative learning involves "learning to work and solve problems in the company of others, and sharpening one's own understanding by listening seriously to the insights of others" (Kuh, 2008, p. 10). One collaborative assignment in our middle grades mathematics methods course is called "Designing Learning Episodes." The goals of this semester-long assignment are for PTs to: (1) learn how to develop and assess mathematics instruction and; (2) learn how to use research-based instructional design practices specific to mathematics to develop, deliver, and assess the impact of their instruction on learners. PTs work in pairs on this assignment and design a sequence of two mathematics lessons using the Launch, Explore, and Summarize format (Serdyukov & Ryan, 2008). This format promotes student-centered approaches for teaching mathematics. Additionally, PTs must collaboratively prepare an assessment plan that outlines the formative and summative assessments for the instructional sequence. The following section provides a description of the parts and sequence of this assignment.

To complete the Designing Learning Episodes assignment, the mathematics methods course instructor scaffolds student learning through a sequence of collaborative tasks and individual work. Figure 1 lists the sequence of tasks and provides a description and purpose of each task.

Collaborative Tasks and Individual Work	Description	Purpose
Collaborative Task 1	PTs are paired based on grade level (6-9) and collaboratively choose a topic from the state standards to use for the Designing Learning Episodes Assignment	To begin the collaboration.
Individual Work 1	PTs complete the following questions adapted from "Thinking Through a Lesson Plan Template [TTLPT]" (Smith, Bill, & Hughes, 2008): Part 1: • What are your mathematical goals for the lesson (what do you want your students to learn)? • What is your rich mathematical task? • What are all the ways the problem can be solved? Part 2: • What questions might you ask students as they work on the task? Part 3: • How will you orchestrate the class discussion, with special attention to accomplishing the mathematical goals determined in Part 1? • How will you know the students have accomplished the mathematical goals? • What are the next steps to build on the learning from this lesson?	To individually brainstorm the content of the lessons.
Collaborative Task 2	PTs discuss the TTLPT, make modifications, and come to an agreement about how the topic will be taught.	To share ideas about how to teach the topic and hypothesize about how student learning might occur. Also, to have time to ask questions and discuss ideas with the course instructor.

Individual Work 2	PTs are introduced to the Launch, Explore, Summarize lesson plan format through watching "Learning to Plan" video (https://connectedmath.msu.edu/teacher-support/support-for-teaching/learning-to-plan/) and then answer the following questions: • How would you describe the significant steps in a teacher's planning process? • In what ways does the teacher plan for the Launch, Explore, and Summarize phases of the lesson?	To gain insight on how a middle school teacher thinks through the launch, explore, summarize parts of lesson planning.
Collaborative Task 3	PTs cooperatively write their lesson plans and assessment plans and the course instructor provides written feedback.	To gain experience lesson planning with a team.
Individual Work 3	PTs individually teach the lessons during their field experience and reflect on each lesson using the following questions (Moss, Bertolone-Smith, & Lamberg, 2017): • What was the mathematical meaning you wanted to occur in this lesson? • What conceptions and misconceptions occurred for the students during the activities? • What situation or activity led to these conceptions and misconceptions? • What student comments and reflections were shared? • What did you change and why? What are you going to do for the next lesson? Why?	To gain experience delivering mathematics instruction and assessing student learning.
Collaborative Task 4	PTs share their experiences and reflections on the lessons.	To debrief and make modifications to the lessons and assessments.

Figure 1. Sequence of tasks for the Designing Learning Episodes assignment.

By completing the Designing Learning Episodes assignment as described in Figure 1, the PTs' final product is two carefully designed lessons. Discussion and collaboration with peers provide PTs with a more comprehensive and detailed vision for their lesson plans. Moreover, PTs are given multiple opportunities to brainstorm about potential student learning, misconceptions, and assessments of student learning. The theory of social constructivism (Vygotsky, 1978) reflects this perspective where the central tenet is that learners construct their own understanding by participating in meaningful shared discourse by which more can be learned through collaboration than independently. The final task of the assignment involves PTs sharing their reflections on their teaching and student learning. Reflection on lessons is essential because it can lead to improved teaching and bring to the forefront ways students are learning the content. The collaborative reflection in this assignment provides PTs with practice on adjusting lessons and realizing that a lesson plan is not a static document to be implemented. We have found that the Designing Learning Episodes assignment works for us and supports collaboration.

References

Cohen, D. K., & Ball, D. L. (1999). *Instruction, capacity, and improvement.* (CPRE Research Report No. RR-043). Retrieved from Study of Instructional Improvement website: http://www.sii.soe.umich.edu/about/pubs.html

Kuh, G. D. (2008). *High-impact educational practices: What they are, who has access to them, and why they matter.* Washington, D.C.: Association of American Colleges and Universities.

Moss, D., Bertolone-Smith, C., & Lamberg, T. (2017). The influence of daily reflection on a middle school teacher's practice. In E. Galindo, & J. Newton (Eds.), *Proceedings of the 38th Annual Meeting of the North American Chapter of the International Group of the Psychology of Mathematics Education (PME-NA)*, Indianapolis, Indiana.

Serdyukov, P., & Ryan, M. (2008). *Writing effective lesson plans: The 5-star approach.* New York, NY: Pearson.

Smith, M., Bill, V., & Hughes, E. (2008). Thinking through a lesson: Successfully implementing high-level tasks. *Mathematics Teaching in the Middle School, 14*(3), 132-138.

Vygotsky, L. (1978). *Mind in society: The development of higher psychological processes.* Cambridge, MA: Harvard University Press.

Diana L. Moss, Appalachian State University
Lisa L. Poling, Appalachian State University
Tracy Goodson-Espy, Appalachian State University
Kathleen Lynch-Davis, Coastal Carolina University

Weaving Collaboration throughout a Course

Some projects necessitate collaboration, and effective collaboration can be an important educational end in itself. I teach a grant writing course that is largely populated by students preparing for human services professions. Grant seeking is notoriously competitive, and teams made up of complementary abilities and perspectives can have an advantage toward successfully acquiring funds. A key objective of the course is for students to experience and practice managing some of the benefits and challenges of collaboration that they will eventually experience in the workforce or in their voluntary efforts. I will describe how I weave collaboration throughout my grant writing course as an illustration of using frequent and diverse forms of collaboration as integral components of a course. Such an approach can be adapted to other courses that can benefit by incorporating collaborative assignments and projects.

At the beginning of the course, I set the stage for frequent collaboration by introducing the course as a workshop in which students practice skills related to acquiring grants while accessing instructor and peer (student) input. I introduce the capstone project for the course, which is a realistic grant application, like those required for federal grants. Several class assignments are linked to that project. Students are directed to consider their own personal and professional interests as they begin to develop a project for which they would need to seek funding. After sharing their interests and tentative project ideas, students form groups based on similar interests. However, at least one member of the team must have a different major (or option or concentration in a major), which helps simulate working with specialized experts toward a common goal. Each team identifies and visits with (preferably in person, though video conferencing is acceptable) a representative from a community agency or organization that engages in work similar to the students' tentative project ideas. In collaboration with the agency, students flesh out realistic details of their project, as if the agency intended to add or expand its services based on the discussion with the students. Projects must entail more than just the addition of physical resources (e.g., updated computers or other equipment) by including new activities or educational components that they will help develop, ensuring that students experience a significant amount of planning and writing related to their project. Students send a copy of their completed grant proposal to the agency as a potential template for a real grant application, should the agency choose to pursue it.

For the majority of the course, and during most of the classroom time, students work on assignments related to the various skills involved with creating a grant proposal. A specific string of graded assignments directly relates to the selected project associated with their grant proposal: a logic model that graphically depicts the components of the project, a concept paper that briefly describes the overall purpose and procedures of the project, a literature review paper that integrates at least five studies that inform the project, and the final grant application with all of its components (a cover sheet, extensive narrative, budget, evaluation plan, timeline, and logic model). A typical class session promotes collaboration by incorporating the following components: students 1) bring in a brief, completed assignment that refers to the assigned reading and objective for the day, 2) work with one or more students to build off of the completed assignment by using course resources to expand and refine their work (e.g., each student creates and brings a basic logic model and works with a partner to blend their ideas and understanding to develop an improved, more expansive model), 3) share the enhanced product with a different student or group who will evaluate and provide feedback based on guidelines I provide during class, 4) further revise work based on the feedback, and 5) highlight their work to the rest of the class. These basic components often vary (e.g., size of groups, number of times get and receive feedback, whether the activity focus is directly on the final grant proposal project or a generic grant writing skill), adding to the variety of collaborative experiences.

Several resources and procedures help promote efficient and substantive classroom collaboration. I request a type of classroom that enables students to quickly and systematically change locations (small tables, chairs with wheels, multiple classroom screens). Such an option is not always available, but I am deliberate about using space and classroom equipment to facilitate active and diverse classroom group engagement. I set up a Google Drive account for the class and create a folder for each team with a corresponding label (I assign a letter to each group, such as "a" through "j"). Students can thus view and simultaneously work on the same documents as individuals and teams. Furthermore, students can view each other's work and provide various levels of peer evaluation. Sometimes the evaluation focuses on ideas and concepts and other times it focuses primarily on writing mechanics. Using Google Drive helps ensure that students receive feedback from everyone throughout the semester (e.g., today students evaluate the work in a Google Drive folder that is located two letters away from their own group; next time they evaluate work in a folder three letters away from their own, and so forth). It can also be used to help keep feedback anonymous (e.g., students evaluate the document in any two folders they choose—or in all the folders) when commenting or making suggested edits for other teams when not engaged in face-to-face collaborative evaluation.

By having regular opportunities to work with other students and to provide each other feedback, and by mixing up the procedures for group work and peer evaluation, students appear to become more comfortable with various forms of collaboration. Students seem invested in each other's work and are thus more engaged in the class. The course as a whole encompasses an overarching spirit of collaboration that facilitates meeting course objectives.

Scott Hall, Ball State University

Pairing High School and College Students So They Can Learn from Each Other

Three years ago, I co-created a collaborative learning activity with a high school teacher, Mr. Michael Tackett. In the semester-long activity, the students in my Psychology and the Law college course and the students in Mr. Tackett's Criminal Justice course become experts in legal and psychological aspects of criminal cases and then share with each other what they have learned.

At the beginning of the semester, Mr. Tackett and I identify six well-known criminal cases (e.g., the Michelle Carter death-by-texting case, infamous serial killer Ted Bundy's case). We split our individual classes into groups of 3-4 students and let every group select which case it wants to study. Throughout the semester, each college student group researches its case's *psychological* aspects (e.g., defendant's background, public opinion of the case), while each high school group investigates its case's *legal* aspects (did the defendant have a guilty mind? what evidence shows the defendant committed various elements of the crime?).

Halfway through the semester, students spend a morning together on the college campus, getting to know one another and sharing what they have learned about their cases. They also determine which group will cover which critical aspects of their cases for the final presentation. Near the semester's end, the college students visit the high school, participating in a 2 ½-hour Research Showcase, in which all 12 groups present what they have learned to one another. For example, for the Boston Bomber Tsarnaev case, this year the college students presented information on the actual crimes committed, then discussed how the brothers' upbringing and growing anti-American attitudes provided the primary motives for the bombing. They were immediately followed by the high school students, who discussed legal elements of the crimes, including how the prosecutors determined which charges to bring forward and what the verdict and sentence for the surviving brother were. Thus, all students were exposed to *both* psychological and legal aspects of all six cases.

Collaborative learning's two primary goals are working with others to solve problems and learning from others' insights (Kuh, 2008). Our students achieve both goals as they work closely with their own group on the research as well as coordinate with their high school counterparts. During the presentations, all students learn psychological and legal information regarding the remaining five cases. Without the collaborative activity, the college students would learn minimal information about the case's legal aspects, while the high school students would learn little about the psychological aspects.

Applying Kuh & O'Donnell's (2013) high impact key elements to this collaborative activity, it seems that all eight of the elements apply. These elements range from submission of smaller assignments throughout the semester (e.g., list of sources for research, project outlines) to a public demonstration of competence (close to 50 people typically attend the showcase).

After the showcase, each college student submits a reflection paper, in which the student shares one's reactions to the collaborative learning activity. Feedback has been overwhelmingly positive. Benefits frequently mentioned include gaining experience researching and synthesizing their case's material, becoming experts on a case they previously knew little about, applying concepts and theories to real cases, doing something different than the typical "write a research paper" assignment, and getting to know their own group members better. Other positive comments were directly related to working with the high school students. Some students noted that they enjoyed getting to know their case's corresponding high school students, working with a group in their community outside of their own school, and serving as mentors and role models to the high school students (e.g., the college students were more effective presenters, and they answered the high school students' questions about college). There were a few negative comments, including some students not wanting to engage in public speaking and not liking group work in general.

Although students haven't addressed the aspect in their reflections, this activity has the additional benefit of giving students the experience of working in teams. The ability to work in a team is repeatedly listed as one of the most important skills college graduates need when entering the workforce (e.g., NACE, 2017). In addition, when students are interviewing for jobs or graduate school spots, they are frequently asked to describe a time they worked on a team or describe a time they experienced conflict and had to resolve it. This collaborative activity is a unique, memorable experience they can share to answer such questions.

This activity could apply to any two disciplines that have a shared topic. For example, English and history classes could collaborate on describing an historic event. The English class' students could share insights into the event based on relevant literature at the time, while the history class' students could research how historians interpreted the event. A strength of this activity is that each group becomes an expert in their area, while getting the benefit of learning from the other area's experts, too. All it takes to get started on this activity is a willing teaching partner and the identification of a topic to which both disciplines could contribute. Simple!

References

Kuh, G.D., & O'Donnell, K. (2013). *Ensuring quality and taking high-impact practices to* scale. Washington, DC: Association of American Colleges and Universities.

Kuh, G.D. (2008). *High-impact educational practices: What they are, who has access to them, and why they matter.* Washington, DC: Association of American Colleges and Universities.

National Association of Colleges and Employers. (2017). *The key attributes employers seek on students' resumes.* https://www.naceweb.org/about-us/press/2017/the-key-attributes-employers-seek-on-students-resumes/

Karyn S. McKenzie, Georgetown College

Student-Organized Speaker Visits: A Diversity of Voices

In many upper-level college classes, students are introduced to research in their fields by reading articles and textbooks written by unknown, unseen writers. Students may feel disconnected or even intimidated by these researcher-writers, not realizing that there is a real human being behind every name. They may also be unaware that science writers and researchers come from diverse backgrounds; yet without a face to connect with the name, students might assume that the individuals who conduct the research they read about form a homogenous group. The reality is far different, and the classroom can be a place to show just that.

How can this issue be tackled in the college classroom? Is it enough to simply point out to students the race and gender of each researcher whose work they learn about, or is there a way to make diversity more tangible and meaningful? One way to show the diversity of voices in a given research field is to invite real researchers to speak with your class directly. And who better to plan and organize these guest speaker visits than the students themselves?

By engaging directly with researchers, students will ideally become more empowered to interact with "big names" and will be inspired to get involved in research themselves. By collaborating in small groups to organize guest visits, students will learn to problem-solve with their classmates in order to facilitate a well-run, intellectually engaging event. Moreover, students will get more personal contact with the invited researchers and will make valuable connections that will serve them in pursuing a career in their field.

In terms of practical considerations, most guest speaker visits can be virtual ones, held via WebEx, Skype, or a similar videoconferencing software. The instructor can initiate the process by first reaching out to known colleagues and collaborators to explain the purpose of the project and to gauge their interest in participating. During this initial step, it is important to cast a wide net and contact researchers who come from a variety of backgrounds so that students can see that experts in their field are as diverse as the research topics they study.

Though each instructor will likely have some idea of what they expect their students to do for such a project, a good first activity with the class is to brainstorm what *they* think the major components of such a visit should be and how they think their efforts should be assessed. For instance, students can contemplate questions like:

- Should the researcher be asked to give a short presentation about their work?
- Should students have read one or more of the researcher's articles prior to the visit?
- Should there be a question-and-answer session, and if so, what types of questions would be appropriate to ask? Who should lead this discussion?
- Is a post-visit write-up a good way to assess students' learning, or would a group discussion better facilitate reflection? Are there other possibilities?
- Finally, how should the responsibilities of organizing the visit by divvied up amongst each group? How should the instructor measure success on this project?

The process of making such decisions as a class engages students more fully in the project. This approach to developing the requirements of the project together also allows for more differentiation in the ways the students can successfully coordinate the speaker visit and in the ways they can demonstrate their learning from the experience.

Colleen Balukas, Ball State University

Team Work Does Not Have To be a Bad Thing

Sometimes students experience a course in ways you do not expect—at least they don't describe it the way you might. Consider this comment a student provided to me on a recent anonymous end-of-semester course evaluation.

> "I liked how the main point of the class was to make ordinarily anti-social, sheltered white young men socialize with each other for the purpose of building rapport showing them team work does not have to be a bad thing."

When I read the comment, my first thought was "that's not what this course is about!" I would describe the same course as being the study of advanced topics and best practices in software development. But, when I took a bit more time to reflect on the student's and my descriptions, I've decided they are not mutually exclusive. In fact, maybe there is even a lot of overlap between them.

This particular course (titled "Advanced Programming") has the students work in small groups for twelve of the fifteen weeks of the semester. The first three weeks are focused on the individual, exposing them to the course content we want them to explore, apply, and internalize the rest of the semester. Then we have a two-week project completed by pairs of students, so they can "test the waters." We provide a detailed explanation of what their program solution is expected to do. At the end of the two weeks, each pair demonstrates to the class what they've been able to accomplish.

The last ten weeks of the semester are devoted to a major project developed by teams of four students. Each team decides what their final project should do, then has to convince me that it can be accomplished in the available time and that it will reasonably fill the available time to complete. Similar to Goldilocks' porridge, it needs to be neither too hot, nor too cold. This final project is delivered in three increments, with each increment being a runnable solution which accomplishes (some of) their goal. Each increment is presented to the class.

This course utilizes a variety of high-impact practices. It involves the students collaboratively working with others toward a common project goal. Further, the final project is delivered in three increments, so there are multiple drafts, each building on the previous. Some time is provided in class for the teams to work together, but the teams are also expected to devote considerable time to the project outside of class. And finally, in-class team presentations of their progress are required. Apparently, this semester it also indirectly touched on diversity issues—at least for one student.

So, let's reflect on the student evaluation mentioned above. I never would have thought to describe the course in this way. Unfortunately, because of the relatively low ethnic and gender diversity in our computer science student body, I cannot say the student is wrong! Interestingly, the thirty-one students enrolled in the course during the semester for which the student provided this comment did have a little ethnic and gender diversity. There were four females, two African Americans, and eight Chinese nationals. Now before you add those up and think that accounts for half of the course enrollment, there was considerable overlap of those three groups. In actuality, more than two-thirds of the students in this section could easily be described as "white young men." And if we were to remove the Chinese students from the calculation, more than ninety percent were "white young men."

Are computer science students "ordinarily anti-social, sheltered white young men"? All too often, this stereotype is true. As with all stereotypes, it is not true of everyone, but usually contains a significant amount of truth. Was the intent of the course to make students "socialize with each other," even if they are not naturally inclined to want to do so? In a sense, yes. One of the major skills computer scientists need to have is the ability to interact with others and to collaboratively work together towards a common goal. Working in pairs and teams is a best practice for computer scientists.

Did we have them work collaboratively "for the purpose of building rapport?" Sure! Collaborative work is much easier if you understand your team members and have established a rapport with them. And lastly, do we want the students to realize that "team work does not have to be a bad thing?" Most definitely. I am sure we've all had bad experiences working collaboratively with others, but that is most likely because the experience was not truly collaborative. We have had that one team member who wants to coast by on our coat tails, or over-commits, and then does not deliver that which they have promised. Learning to deal positively with these situations is an important skill to develop. Working collaboratively—especially with a diverse team that brings different skills and experiences to bear on the group task—allows for more creativity and productivity than any group can hope to achieve as individuals.

So, did the opening student quote capture the essence of the course? At one level, yes. Causing students to learn to work together when they are not inclined to do so and then discovering how successful they likely will be together could certainly fit my course description of "the study of advanced topics and best practices in software development." We certainly have many other, more technically advanced topics and best practices we want the students to learn during the course, but without the ability to work collaboratively, how much good will come of that technical knowledge? Helping students learn the great benefits of collaboratively working together is something we all need to be striving for, regardless of what course we are teaching. Take time to consider how you can incorporate group work into your course and help create future employees who can be an asset to their organization. Maybe then you can have one of your students declare "team work does not have to be a bad thing."

David L. Largent, Ball State University

Introducing Students to Tools to Support Collaboration

For today's students, learning how to collaborate, both in solving problems as a team and in learning from others, is an essential skill. Collaboration is essential for building many of the amazing technologies that we interact with every day. The need for collaboration is not new, as John Donne said in the 17th century, "no man is an island." The challenge is that we are still not that good at it. While the latest *Pulse of the Profession* report from the Project Management Institute (2017) sees evidence of improvement, it still finds that organizations waste an average of $97 million for every $1 billion invested, due to poor project performance. A study (Geneca, 2011) of Information Technology (IT) projects found that among business and IT executives "75% of respondents admit that their projects are either always or usually 'doomed right from the start.'" By helping students develop the skills needed to successfully complete collaborative assignments and projects, we, as educators, are preparing them to support successful collaboration outside the classroom.

Success in collaborative assignments and projects depends on many factors. Amongst these are communication and the use of technologies that support collaboration. Lam (2015) finds that communication quality is a key factor in reducing non-contributing team members. A number of other studies (e.g., Arkilic, Peker, and Uyar 2013 and Davidson 2015) have explored how technology tools can be used to improve communication. There are a wide range of tools available to support communication in collaborative assignments and projects. Modern Learning Management Systems (LMSs), for example, contain many useful tools, often with the ability to make them available to a specific group of students. However, students may not be aware of these tools, or may not have experience using them.

I address this situation with a short group assignment whereby students explore the collaboration tools provided by the LMS used at my university. There are two goals for the assignment. First, students gain knowledge about the group tools provided in the LMS. Students then use this knowledge to reflect on how they might use these tools for the group assignments in the course. Students receive the assignment on the first day of class. The assignment is introduced as part of an in-class discussion about the group assignments and projects that will be part of the class, but no class time is allocated for work on the assignment. Much of the class work on collaborative assignments and projects will need to be done outside of class meetings, so this assignment is not treated any differently.

For the assignment, I use the LMS to randomly create groups of 4 – 5 students. Each group has a separate group area within the LMS that provides a home page and a set of collaboration tools, including the ability to make announcements, hold online group discussions, create wiki pages, share files, and participate in an online video conference. The assignment is published in the LMS with the required activities and submissions along with links to the LMS vendor's documentation on the group tools. For the assignment, students explore the features of each of the tools and get experience by using them to collaborate with other members of their group. An initial suggestion is offered that online discussion tools could be used to arrange a time for the video conference. The instructor has access to all of the group areas, so it is easy to verify the participation of individual students. In addition to exploring the tools, each student submits a written statement that discusses the tools – how hard or easy they were to use – and reflects on how they think these tools could be used in future groups assignments in the course.

Student participation in the assignment provides experience with using the LMS provided collaboration tools, and students readily make use of the tools in later assignments. The student reflections about the use of the collaboration tools show good insight about how the tools can support collaboration. A further impact of the assignment was seen in assignments where students took the initiative to create their own groups in the LMS when they were not provided by the instructor.

References

Arkilic, I. G., Peker, S., & Uyar, M. E. (2013). Students' preferences of communication tools for group projects in a computer-supported collaborative learning environment: A survey. *Procedia – Social and Behavioral Sciences*, 83(2013), 1121-1125.

Davidson, R. (2015). Wiki use that increases communication and collaboration motivation. *Journal of Learning Design*, 8(3), 92-105.

Geneca. (2011). Why up to 75% of software projects will fail. Retrieved January 04, 2018, from https://www.geneca.com/blog/software-project-failure-business-development

Lam, C. (2015). The Role of Communication and Cohesion in Reducing Social Loafing in Group Projects. *Business and Professional Communication Quarterly*, 78(4), 454-475.

Project Management Institute. (2017). *Pulse of the Profession 2017*. Retrieved January 04, 2018, from https://www.pmi.org/learning/thought-leadership/pulse/pulse-of-the-profession-2017

David Woods, Miami University, Hamilton Campus

V. Undergraduate Research

The following are characteristics of this HIP:
- Undergraduate research isn't just for science students.
- All disciplines can engage their students in systematic investigation and research.
- Students' excitement grows as they are involved with a discipline's key questions, research methodologies, and the use of appropriate technology.

This section contains seven articles. If your discipline already utilizes students in research, do they work under or with instructors? If your discipline doesn't have a student research component, why not?

Scholarly & Creative Undergraduate Learning Partnership Team (SCULPT): Triple Areas of Focus

Inquiry Based Learning (IBL), inside and outside the classroom, includes research, scholarship, and creative activity. It is imperative for retaining and engaging students in higher education (Kuh, 2008), particularly at teaching institutions, because it is robust and effective. A key factor is developing faculty-student mentoring relationships beginning early in a students' educational career. This tip focuses on undergraduate research (UR) as an engaged pedagogy with application across all disciplines.

Via a Title III grant, Utah Valley University sent four faculty groups to Council on Undergraduate Research (CUR) training in 2014-2015 on the topics of: Beginning Research Program in Natural Science, Institutionalizing UR, UR in the Social Sciences, and Integrating UR into Curriculum. The Institutionalizing UR faculty group worked to implement it formally and broadly upon their return. A series of meetings to create an organizational strategy resulted in the determination that a recognized and ongoing affinity group needed to be created to promote and implement best practices. From this task, the Scholarly and Creative Undergraduate Learning Team known as SCULPT was born in 2016.

SCULPT is a resource for teaching through IBL. It provides resources for developing inquiry-based pedagogy, encouraging undergraduate research, developing programs, mentoring students, developing skills and traits in students, and helping identify and pursue funding. Essentially, SCULPT was developed as a liaison/advisory group to help allocate academic resources and make them accessible to faculty and undergraduate students.

Utah Valley University and SCULPT therein determined there are three key areas of faculty focus when working to encourage scholarly and creative undergraduate research. These include: first, institutionalization of UR and IBL; second, integration into the curriculum; and third, advocacy–to support the other two areas. Currently, SCULPT is in the first stages of institutionalization with the support of Title III funds to provide training for mentoring students and mini-grants for materials needed in the classroom for engaging in scholarly and creative activities.

Institutionalization Undergraduate Research and Inquiry-Based Learning

IBS is essential to the development of highly skilled professionals and productive adults. When combined with other traditional educational opportunities, undergraduate research helps in developing and preparing students for successful career paths after graduation. "Undergraduate research is like role-playing. I mean no disparagement of the research -- role-playing is a critical part of life. Children learn how to be adults in part by trying on grown-up clothes and imitating a parent who is, say, driving a car or vacuuming a rug. Similarly, undergraduates can learn the conventions of research through imitation and practice" (Chapman, 2003, para. 7). It is often said that 'practice makes perfect,' but it is probably better said that practice makes prepared. "Through guided participation and extensive collaboration, long-term observation and practice, the novice researcher gradually acquires the skills and expertise needed for effective performance in the profession" (Adedokun, Dyehouse, Bessenbacher, & Burgess, 2010, p. 3).

To establish a stronger engaged learning enterprise, SCULPT identified tactics that included training faculty as research mentors, developing research collaboratives, and advancing the concept of research and creative activities as pedagogy. For these purposes, the Mentoring Academy was created. This is an activity group which helps faculty establish their UR projects. SCULPT also promotes interdisciplinary collaboration and projects on targeted issues.

Advancing the concept of research and creative activities as pedagogy is critical. Central to the concept of IBL as a form of engaged pedagogy is the instructor role in the design of students' scholarly and creative experiences, the integration and preparation of student skill development leading towards competence and autonomy in selecting their own questions or goals for their work, and the active use of best practices and student learning outcomes to shape the student experience. Through these relationships, faculty can set professional expectations, assist students in applying the concepts they have been learning in their coursework, encourage problem-solving and autonomy, and more. Students are also encouraged to showcase their results in local and national conferences where they receive feedback from their peers with the ultimate goal of publishing their findings.

Integration into the Curriculum

To impact retention, students need to be involved in research early and often. "Students, who participate in research early, during the first year and second year, are more likely to succeed and graduate with college degrees in STEM disciplines. Such students are also likely to advance to graduate school in STEM areas or proceed to professional schools" (Fakayode, Yakubu, Adeyeye, Pollard, & Mohammed, 2014, p. 663). This relationship is not only true of STEM disciplines. Integration needs to occur across a variety of departments, courses, and academic levels.

Universities need to broaden access to undergraduate research opportunities. These opportunities are often reserved for the students who have proven to excel. Haave and Audet (2013) encourage institutions to not only focus on high achievers: "Our data reveals that the majority of students with lower than average GPA earned relatively high grades in those research courses, hence receiving accrued benefits from the experience… Admission to [Undergraduate Research Experiences (UREs)] based only on prior GPA thus appears to be counter-productive by denying access to high impact educational experiences from students who would most benefit from it" (p. 4). This finding is significant for open admission universities such as ours where the opportunity to engage in undergraduate research experience enables students to develop the necessary skills for current market conditions.

Advocacy – to Support the Other Two Areas

Encouragement and incorporation of IBL require consistent and intentional effort, especially when campus resources and opportunities are strained. Collaboration with other offices throughout the university has been key for SCULPT goals and projects. These opportunities should not be wholly extracurricular but integrated into the standard curriculum because they prepare graduates to be successful. For this reason, the third focus area is fundamental for the long-term sustainability of the project. By creating a culture and structures supportive of inquiry-based learning and by expanding the reach of IBL to all students on campus, the institution's dedication to student engagement, inclusion, rigor, and student success will be enhanced.

References

Adedokun, O. A., Dyehouse, M. Bessenbacher, A., & Burgess, W. D. (2010, April). Exploring faculty perceptions of the benefits. Paper presented at the Annual Meeting of the American Educational Research Association, Denver, CO. Retrieved from http://files.eric.ed.gov/fulltext/ED509729.pdf

Chapman, D. W. (2003). Undergraduate research: Showcasing young scholars. *The Chronicle of Higher Education*. Retrieved from http://chronicle.com/article/Undergraduate-Research-/9284

Fakayode, S. O., Yakubu, M., Adeyeye, O. M., Pollard, D. A., & Mohammed, A. K. (2014). Promoting undergraduate STEM education at a historically black college and university through research experience. *Journal of Chemical Education, 91*(5), 662–665. doi: 10.1021/ed400482b.

Haave, N. & Audet, D. (2013). Evidence in support of removing boundaries to undergraduate research experience. *Collected essays on learning and teaching*, 6, 105-110. Retrieved from http://celt.uwindsor.ca/ojs/leddy/index.php/CELT/article/viewFile/3737/3081

Kuh, G.D. (2008). Excerpt from high-impact educational practices: What they are, who has access to them, and why they matter. Retrieved from the Association of American Colleges & Universities website: https://www.aacu.org/leap/hips

Dr. Anne Arendt, Utah Valley University
Dr. Ana Aguilera, Utah Valley University
Dr. Maritza Sotomayor, Utah Valley University
Dr. Anton Tolman, Utah Valley University
Dr. Olga Kopp, Utah Valley University

Opening the Doors of Research Laboratories to All

Although research opportunities are becoming more common in all universities, larger state universities are oftentimes not as effective in recruiting students for labs, or in adequately disseminating information about their labs to students. Solely expecting students to seek out such knowledge can be problematic because oftentimes students don't know that such opportunities exist, don't know research can be helpful for their careers, and even develop misconceptions about research that deter them from seeking out more information. Adedokun and Burgess (2011) studied students' preconceived ideas about laboratory research prior to student participation in such labs. They found that many undergraduate students expected the research environment to be stern and lacking in social interaction. Furthermore, they expected professors running laboratories to fit the stereotypical image of hard-nosed scientists. Many students also expected high levels of group work instead of more independent research.

These preconceptions were directly contradictory to how undergraduate students actually experienced the lab once they began to participate. Adedokun and Burgess (2011) found that students who participated in labs began to value research more highly. They also particularly enjoyed experiences in laboratory environments that were socially warm and provided opportunities for active participation in research. This study highlights why just expecting students to seek out research opportunities is a poor recruitment strategy. Sadly, students who want to continue with a graduate education typically don't realize the importance of such research experiences until they actually apply to graduate programs.

To improve the passive recruitment strategy commonly used by many large universities, professors should provide clear information to students. Students specifically need to know that such opportunities do indeed exist, what they expect of laboratories may not be accurate, and the many benefits to their careers if they choose to participate in undergraduate research. Such laboratory participation helps not only students with goals of attending graduate school, but also students who are more career-minded and want to begin work immediately after college. An easy way to communicate this information is to advertise current research opportunities. Advertising is most effective when done in multiple formats, including frequently discussing opportunities in the classroom, emailing students about opportunities, and sharing information about the benefits of research experience in the syllabus, or better yet, requiring some laboratory research experience as a class requirement. Such a multi-prong approach counteracts the tendency to handpick certain students who seem like good fits, and instead disseminate information to a broader array of students who are taking classes in areas such as psychology, biology, or chemistry.

Research by Taraban and Logue (2012) suggests that although professors should have benchmarks for participation in undergraduate research, such as a high GPA, those with lower GPAs who may need to learn time management or study strategies can still benefit from research if given the right support. Successful undergraduate research programs allow a wide range of students to participate in research, especially those who represent underrepresented minorities or first-generation college students. Students from marginalized backgrounds are particularly likely to lack the self-confidence to seek out research experiences and may be overwhelmed at the numerous independent steps required to initiate such research (Mennella, 2015). These steps include initiating an undergraduate research project, selecting an undergraduate advisor, and approaching the faculty member about the possibility of doing research.

To truly create a course that meaningfully integrates undergraduate research experience, Mennella (2015) recommends the following suggestions. The lab course must contain an experimental project that requires a number of steps to be completed over a significant period of time; experimental failures need to be expected and planned for; experimental tests, controls, and/or validations must be embedded into the overall project to verify that the project is progressing as intended and planned; and all students must be synchronized so that all students are working on the same steps during the same class-period. Mennella (2015) states that this type of design has shown to "provide students with a genuine and bona fide research experience as part of their regular scheduled course load" (p. 530). These steps can help expand students' skillsets and mindsets by exposing them to the kind of real research that really matters.

References

Mennella, T. A. (2015). Designing authentic undergraduate research experiences in a single-semester lab course. *American Biology Teacher, 77*(7), 526-531.

Adedokun, O. A., & Burgess, W. D. (2011). Uncovering students' preconceptions of undergraduate research experiences. *Journal of STEM Education: Innovations & Research, 12*(5/6), 12-22.

Taraban, R., & Logue, E. (2012). Academic factors that affect undergraduate research experiences. *Journal of Educational Psychology, 104*(2), 499-514. doi:10.1037/a0026851

Ameenah Ikram, Spalding University

Involving Undergraduate Students in Research

Thinking back to my undergraduate education, I realize one of my most memorable and valuable experiences was being involved in a research lab. I learned more in this laboratory than I learned in almost all of my basic required classes. I was fortunately able to join a lab during my first year of college—an opportunity not available to many first-year students. Working with my classmates and professor in a laboratory setting created a breadth of opportunities because I had time to learn the lower level research skills first, then build on these skills the following three years. I began as a research assistant, learned coding and entering data, and eventually became a researcher for an independent study that was submitted for publication before graduation. Without guidance from my faculty mentor and the opportunity to participate in research, I would have missed out on a tremendous learning experience.

Friedrich (2014) noted that engaging freshman and sophomore students in research can be challenging because of their limited skill level and experience in a field, but developed an approach to involve these students. This approach was similar to my hierarchical experience in research, which exposed student researchers to data collection, quality evaluation, interpretation, and presentation of results (Friedrich, 2014) in a focused, sequential manner. Upper level students not only conducted their own research, but also mentored younger students in the research process. Early engagement in research opportunities, when carefully scaffolded, has the potential to provide rich learning experiences, as well as help students pursue more advanced degrees.

Sears, Boyce, Boon, Goghari, Irwin, and Boyes (2017) found that opportunities to engage in research are a key contributor to student satisfaction in a psychology undergraduate degree program. Research in other fields has supported the importance of engaging in research for engineering students, finding that engineering students who participate in research report higher skill levels in engineering as well as communication (Carter, Ro, Alcott, & Lattuca, 2016). These findings support the notion that research is important not only in a classroom setting, but it teaches skills that are generalizable outside of the classroom and contribute to students' ultimate success in their chosen fields.

Sometimes students develop an imposter syndrome, making them hesitant to seek out research opportunities (Christensen, Aubeeluck, Fergusson, Craft, Knight, Wirihana, & Stupple, 2016). Students often believe that their achievement is not due to their own ability or acquired skills, but instead due to luck or the belief that they work harder than other individuals. Individuals with imposter syndrome feel as though they are frauds and fear that they are not as competent as other individuals. Peteet, Montgomery, and Weekes (2015) found that students who had higher levels of imposter syndrome were often dissatisfied with life and themselves overall. Imposter syndrome is particularly common among students of color at predominantly white institutions (Solórzano, Ceja, & Yosso, 2000). This research points to the need for professors to reach out to all students, and especially reach out directly and actively to students of color.

The key to creating a university culture of research is to make these research experiences readily available to all students. The single reason that I got involved with research so early is that I was approached and invited to join a research lab by my faculty mentor. Unfortunately, other students see the benefits of joining a research lab when they are seniors and applying to graduate schools. Seniors are typically not able to gain the full set of skills and experiences compared to students who have participated in a laboratory experience for several years. As such, they are less likely to start an independent research project that has the potential to be published. In summary, laboratory experiences work because they enable students to gain richer learning opportunities compared to the conventional learning experiences acquired in the classroom, leading to eventual greater success in their chosen field.

References

Carter, D. F., Ro, H. K., Alcott, B., & Lattuca, L. R. (2016). Co-curricular connections: The role of undergraduate research experiences in promoting engineering students' communication, teamwork, and leadership skills. *Research in Higher Education, 57*(3), 363-393.

Christensen, M., Aubeeluck, A., Fergusson, D., Craft, J., Knight, J., Wirihana, L., & Stupple, E. (2016). Do student nurses experience imposter phenomenon? An international comparison of final year undergraduate nursing students' readiness for registration. *Journal of Advanced Nursing, 72*(11), 2784-2793.

Friedrich, J. M. (2014). A classroom-based distributed workflow initiative for the early involvement of undergraduate students in scientific research. *Journal of Science Education and Technology, 23*(1), 59-66.

Peteet, B., Montgomery, L., & Weekes, J. C. (2015). Predictors of imposter phenomenon among talented ethnic minority undergraduate students. *Journal of Negro Education, 84*(2), 175-186.

Sears, C. R., Boyce, M. A., Boon, S. D., Goghari, V. M., Irwin, K., & Boyes, M. (2017). Predictors of student satisfaction in a large psychology undergraduate program. *Canadian Psychology/Psychologie Canadienne, 58*(2), 148-160.

Solórzano, D., Ceja, M., & Yosso, T. (2000). Critical race theory, racial microaggressions, and campus racial climate: The experiences of African American college students. *Journal of Negro Education, 69*(1-2), 60-73.

Michaela Herbig, Spalding University

An Interview Project for the Arts Classroom

In my 20th- and 21st-century music history class, I was worried that students were not getting adequate exposure to the kind of work composers are doing today. A historical textbook cannot address ongoing developments, while a traditional curriculum focused on knowledge acquisition and assessment will inevitably fail to communicate the vibrant diversity of contemporary music. I tackled this problem by creating a research project for which my students each interview a young composer, study one of his or her works, and present their findings in a public forum. Although I conduct this project in a music class, it would be equally successful in any discipline that deals with the creative products of modern society, including art, drama, literature, or poetry.

I begin by asking my students to listen to a variety of works submitted by composers who have agreed to participate in the project. They select their favorites and write short responses, which allows me to pair students with composers who interest them. Next, the students prepare to interview their composers. We brainstorm questions in class and discuss the different aspects of a composer's professional and creative life that are worth investigating, including career path, sources of income, inspirations, artistic philosophy, and education. Students also develop questions about the specific work that they have been assigned. Following the interview, which takes place via phone or video chat, the students submit interview reflections, thesis statements, and paper outlines. This process allows them to practice different modes of writing and guides them to develop a strong final product. The regular deadlines also keep students on track and provide lots of opportunities for feedback. The final papers, which combine information and insight from the interviews with additional research and an original analysis of the assigned work, each make a coherent argument about music composition today. I meet with every student to discuss their paper draft and slides at least once. The final presentations are open to the campus community, and each is followed by a period of discussion.

This project has entirely satisfied my initial concern. On the one hand, every student gets exposure to a wide variety of works that, taken together, represent most of the current trends in music composition. After sharing their discoveries with one another, each student leaves the class with a good idea about how composers today make a living, what kinds of art music are being produced, and where the future of composition might lie. On the other hand, I am able to introduce diversity into a curriculum that has historically been dominated by white men. The composers I recruit to participate in this project come from a variety of backgrounds and include women and people of color, and their voices contribute a great deal to my students' conceptions of who a composer might be and what the work entails. Our best presentation-driven discussions have dealt with the topics of representation and opportunity for those who have long been excluded from the field.

This project also creates an excellent opportunity for arts students to complete meaningful original research. In the past, several of my students have presented their work at the National Conference for Undergraduate Research, an experience that would not otherwise have been available to them. Some of my students have also submitted their work to be published in an undergraduate research journal. In 2017, I joined with the composition professor at my institution to organize a formal conference, and my students presented their work on campus alongside visiting researchers and performers. This project compels students to make original contributions to the field of music history. In this way, they learn not by internalizing the work of other musicologists but by becoming musicologists themselves.

Esther M. Morgan-Ellis, University of North Georgia

A Research Laboratory Course as a High-Impact Practice

The benefits of undergraduate research as a high-impact student experience cannot be overstated. Put simply, undergraduate students who engage in research either as part of a course, working with a team of undergraduates, or on an independent research project not only show increases in their understanding of research, but also develop interest in careers that involve research (e.g., Russell, Hancock, & McCullough, 2007). Ample data (e.g., Lopatto, 2012) attest to its value with regard to self-reported gains in disciplinary skills, professional advancement, personal development, and intellectual skills.

Additional research points to the importance and benefits of undergraduate research. For example, Petrella and Jung (2008) report on the success of requiring all students in a major to complete an independent research project in their senior year. In a study about whether introductory psychology courses benefit advanced students, Nathanson, Paulhus, and Williams (2004) found that adding a laboratory course encourages students to perceive of psychology as a science. Thieman, Clary, Olson, Dauner, and Ring (2009) found that including a research laboratory component to their introductory psychology course increased students' knowledge of and comfort level with scientific approaches, as well as scientific literacy.

Recognizing the myriad benefits of undergraduate research, we designed a one-credit hour course titled "Foundational Experiences" that is taken concurrently with Introduction to Psychology (three credit hours). The primary goals of the course are to instill in students the value of research in psychology and to provide an opportunity for hands-on experience with a research project. The laboratory course has four modules: Getting Started, Research Consumer, Research Participant, and Research Producer. The student learning outcomes of the course include:

1. Articulate why the processes of scientific inquiry and critical thinking are important for psychological research and practice.
2. Describe the process of psychological research and identify key elements of research (e.g., informed consent) and variations in research methods (e.g., qualitative versus quantitative research; experimental versus correlational research).
3. Identify the core competencies (areas of knowledge, skills, and self/other awareness) of psychological scientists and relate them to academic and non-academic career paths within and outside psychology.
4. Recognize the implications of personal and professional ethical principles as a member of the University, professional, and global communities.

The table below shows each of the modules and their associated module student learning outcomes.

Module	Student Learning Outcome
Getting Started	• Identify the types of research activities we will engage in during the course • Articulate the steps in the research process
Research Consumer	• Describe a famous experiment/study to a lay audience • Construct a display (mini poster) of the famous psychologist and/or experiment/study
Research Participant	• Articulate your experiences as a participant in research • Articulate the value of participating in research
Research Producer	• Search the scientific literature • Summarize research articles • Collect survey data • Analyze survey data • Produce an APA research report

Below, we describe each of the modules that we designed to allow students to achieve these learning outcomes.

In the *Getting Started* module, we provide students with an overview of the course in general and of the importance of research in psychology in particular. We ask students to view a video about the value of research in psychology and to read a chapter about survey research. For each activity, they are required to complete a worksheet that allows them to report and reflect on their learning.

The primary goal of the *Research Consumer* module is to provide opportunities for students to gain experience as critical consumers of psychological research. We ask students, in three consecutive weeks, to choose three cases from the "Forty studies that changed psychology" text (Hock, 2013) and construct mini posters that describe the famous study. We ask them to discuss the historical importance of the study in a manner that could easily be understood by a layperson.

In the *Research Participant* module, we ask students, in three consecutive weeks, to choose three online studies in which to participate, and then complete worksheets reporting their experience and what they learned about research. Note that we provide students with an equivalent option if they choose not to participate in a study.

Finally, in the *Research Producer* module, we ask students to complete a research project to test the hypothesis that people are happy. In the first assignment, we guide students through the process of searching the scholarly literature for research about happiness. They are required to submit a worksheet that reports on the process and results of their literature search. In the second assignment, students read a journal article about a study on happiness and then complete a worksheet that asks them to report on the hypothesis, method, results, and limitations of the study. For the third assignment, we ask students to collect data from at least 10 participants. They are given the Oxford Happiness Survey (Argyle, Martin, & Crossland, 1989), but they decide if they want to collect data via paper-and-pencil or to use an electronic method. The fourth assignment involves analysis of the data. In this step, we ask students to submit their data in an Excel file and compute the mean happiness score for each respondent, as well as the overall mean. In the last step, we ask students to write a mini APA-style manuscript of the study.

At the end of the course, we ask students to complete a research reflection assignment with the following student learning outcomes:
- To be able to describe what you learned about research
- To be able to explain the value of research in psychology

This assignment provides students with the opportunity to reflect on how each of the modules built on one another to provide them with an opportunity to experience research as a consumer, participant, and producer.

References

Argyle, M., Martin, M., & Crossland, J. (1989). Happiness as a function of personality and social encounters. In J. P. Forgas, & J. M. Innes (Eds.), *Recent advances in social psychology: An International perspective* (pp. 189–203). North-Holland: Elsevier.

Hock, R. R. (2013). *Forty studies that changed psychology* (7th ed.). Upper Saddle River, N.J.: Pearson/Prentice Hall.

Lopatto, D. (2010). Undergraduate research as a high-impact student experience. *Peer Review, 12(2)*, 27-30.

Nathanson, C., Paulhus, D. L., & Williams, K. M. (2004). The challenge to cumulative learning: do introductory courses actually benefit advanced students? *Teaching of Psychology*, 31(1), 5–9. http://doi.org/10.1207/s15328023top3101_2.

Petrella, J. K, Jung, A. P. (2008). Undergraduate Research: Importance, Benefits, and Challenges. *International Journal of Exercise Science*, 1(3), 91–95.

Russell S. H., Hancock M. P., McCullough J.(2007). Benefits of undergraduate research experiences. *Science*, 316, 548-549.

Thieman, T. J., Clary, E. G., Olson, A. M., Dauner, R. C., & Ring, E. E. (2009). Introducing students to psychological research: general psychology as a laboratory course. *Teaching of Psychology*, 36(3), 160–168. http://doi.org/10.1080/00986280902959994.

Beth Dietz, Miami University
Barbara B. Oswald, Miami University

Developing a Collegial Relationship with Undergraduate Research Students

When I [Robyn] was an undergraduate, I began doing research with my faculty because I thought it would help me be admitted to graduate school. Some projects I enjoyed; some I did not. For most projects, I felt like I was annoying the faculty member who had to take time out of their busy schedule to assign me tasks or to direct me to a graduate student who would assign me tasks. Only rarely was I part of a research team where I understood the prior literature, the hypotheses of the current study, and the methodology of the current study.

Upon becoming a professor, I understood better why some of my professors appeared to be annoyed and admired those who were able to incorporate undergraduate students into their research team. Working with undergraduates on research projects requires enormous amounts of time and patience. In many cases, the process of conducting research can be slowed by including undergraduates who may have little to no understanding of the research process. In spite of these drawbacks, engaging students in research can help them in myriad ways: develop their interest in conducting research, develop knowledge on specific topics in psychology, enhance their application to graduate school, develop skills leading to jobs, and help them identify areas of interest.

For me, the question became how do I *balance* my own needs as a professor (institutional requirements for publishing as well as enriching my desire to learn and contribute) with engaging students in a coherent undergraduate research experience that meets their needs. The solution developed across many years of trial and error. When students approach me regarding participating in research, I follow a multi-step process:

- Step One: I meet individually with the student to discover their goals. Are they interested in working with me on one of my projects, or are they interested in developing an independent project? Are they interested in graduate school? What is their understanding of the research process? Have they completed a research methods course? Have they worked with any other professor on research projects? For most students, this initial interview takes only about ten to fifteen minutes. Students without prior research experience frequently have little idea of what to expect and assume they will work on one of my research projects.

- Step Two: At the end of the initial interview, I make a decision whether I think I could work with this student. I'm fairly flexible about working with students and tend to turn away only those who are disrespectful during this initial interview. For all other students, I'm willing to invest time and energy into their development. However, I tell students that to work with me, we both need to sign my Research Agreement document. This document outlines my expectations of the student and what the student can expect from me.
  - My expectations of students:
    - Complete all tasks as assigned
    - Ask if something is unclear
    - Maintain confidentiality about research
  - What students can expect from me:
    - Prompt response (within 24 hours) to all questions/emails
    - Tasks assigned according to their demonstrated abilities
    - Discussion of co-authorship on any presentations or publications when their contributions warrant it

  Students are frequently surprised by this open discussion of their responsibilities and the responsibilities that I, as the instructor, have toward them. I have found this open discussion at the start of the relationship eliminates confusion and upset later.
- Step Three: The student and I work together to determine which research project is the best match for their interests and skills. Although students may be most interested in Project X, that project may be at a stage where the student's current skills are not appropriate. Project Y, while less interesting, may allow students to work at a level appropriate for their skills. Skill levels I address with students include:
  - Review of the literature: Students with little to no prior research experience will most likely start here. Students conduct searches relating to particular topics, download articles into an electronic folder (I use Box folders), and provide summaries of each article. All students wishing to conduct an independent project will begin at this stage.
  - Collecting data: Although collecting data may seem like a relatively low-level skill, I expect all students involved in data collection to have a thorough understanding of the research literature relating to the study. Students who collect data for a study will receive a footnote in any future publications but not co-authorship.
  - Design: Students at this level will be involved in discussions about designing the next study in a research area, including crafting the IRB documents

and writing hypotheses. Students who assist in designing a study will be given co-authorship in any future presentation or publication.
- Data Analysis: Students at this level must have completed a methods course and be proficient in using SPSS. Students who assist in data analysis will be given co-authorship in any future presentation or publication.
- Final Write-ups: This is the highest level of research participation for my students, requiring that students be excellent writers, familiar with APA format, and capable of integration. Students who assist in the write-up of a study will be given co-authorship in any future presentation or publication.

This approach to working with undergraduate research students has resulted in a small research team with students at different stages of development. The interactions between these students vary tremendously from semester to semester, depending upon their schedules and their skill levels. Ideally, a single time for all research students to meet with me every two weeks could be scheduled. Practically, I meet with individual students or smaller groups of students who are working on the same project.

The approach I've developed works well. I'm less frustrated with students as they are not assigned tasks that are beyond their skill levels. Students understand that, as they demonstrate advanced skills, there is a pathway clearly outlined for them to become more active in research, leading to co-authorship on presentations and publications.

Robin K. Morgan, Indiana University Southeast
Nathanael Mitchell, Spalding University

Facilitating Research Engagement and Student Success

Academics have consistently cited research as the catalyst for student success (Anderson, Bonds-Raacke, & Raacke, 2015). Students who conduct research enjoy enhanced learning experiences, increased retention, increased enrollment in graduate institutions, mentoring relationships with faculty, and more effective preparation for the workforce (The Council on Undergraduate Research, 2011). Similarly, research experience is referenced as the top deciding factor for competitive employment positions and entrance into graduate programs (Norcross, 2014).

Despite the multitude of benefits of engaging in research, many students choose not to participate. Why don't students take advantage of research opportunities, and how can we overcome their barriers to participation? Despite the often-touted "too much work, not enough time" explanation offered by students, we hypothesized that students faced other barriers to engaging in research. Students across universities both big and small have similar workloads, high levels of stress and demanding deadlines, but some students schedule time to engage in research and some do not. Understanding student barriers to research is critical so that faculty can better address and remove these challenges.

In order to discover what prohibits student participation in research groups and what encourages participation at our own institution, we surveyed the students themselves in a brief qualitative survey. We asked the students only three questions. The first question asked students to list, aside from time constraints and excessive demands, factors that prohibited their involvement in research. The second question asked students to identify positive factors that were crucial to facilitating their research involvement. The third question asked whether the relationship between the student and the faculty member conducting research was an influencing factor to research involvement and contribution, and, if so, what was it about the relationship that influenced their decision?

Despite the obvious barrier of time restraints, students reported several other barriers to research participation. An overwhelming number of students reported pure *lack of awareness of available opportunities*. Others explained that the *lack of confidence in their ability to be successful,* combined with the competitive nature of research, actively deters them from participating in opportunities. One student explained that *competition between students* "makes research unnecessarily stressful and takes the enjoyment out of it." Furthermore, without prior experience, students noted just the idea of embarking on research projects can be overwhelming. A lack of support from faculty and peers can lead to students feeling inadequate and overwhelmed with the process, interfering with their ability to complete assigned projects. Additionally, many students reported that when faculty requirements to remain a part of a research team become *too demanding (i.e., requiring a specific number of publications or presentations per year)*, they tend to withdraw from these research opportunities.

Although identifying barriers to research is extremely helpful, understanding motivating factors is equally important. We wanted to understand what motivates some students to seek out research opportunities, while others do not. If we can identify some of the common motivating factors, perhaps we can expand these motivational factors to encourage other students to increase their research participation.

Respondents reported that *consistent meetings* in which professors, peers, and other professionals discuss research opportunities and ideas are vital to keeping students informed and encouraging involvement. Students also reported appreciating opportunities to *"twist" research opportunities to their individual topics of interest.* Students prefer a *wide array of research opportunities*, from large, ongoing grant-funded studies (with the goal of being published in tier one research journal publications) to smaller "quick hit" short-term scholarship projects (with the goal of being published in less prestigious journals). *Flexible time commitments and manageable workloads* are also important. This flexibility allows students to choose research projects that fit their schedule and workload. Being able to *collaborate with peers* on certain projects also decreases the workload, making even small projects more manageable.

However, overwhelmingly, the singular identified crucial factor that students reported contributing to their research engagement was faculty encouragement and support. Students reported that their relationship with a faculty member was the deal breaker/deal maker as to whether to get involved in research. Students explained they must *"trust" the faculty person* with whom they work. Successful professors were described as *motivating, encouraging, genuine, and enthusiastic.* These professors instill confidence and *"encourage participation without pressuring."* Encouraging individual research interests is also desired. Professors should also be aware of the student's ability level, providing *scaffolding in developmentally appropriate levels* to help students succeed. Beginning-level students cited heavy professor guidance as helpful, while more advanced students appreciated the autonomy allowed by their mentors. The professor must also provide *realistic goals and deadlines*. Providing *prompt feedback* throughout the process allows goals and deadlines to be met with ease and minimal last-minute stress. Students also appreciate *professors who are receptive to feedback* and can *work collaboratively with the student.* Numerous students noted that *just being able to develop relationships with a faculty member motives them* to become more involved in the research.

In short, successful student-faculty collaborations begin with successful student-faculty relationships. Faculty must work to overcome barriers that restrict students' research participation. Lack of opportunities, confidence, and support can be resolved by a professor who is willing to work to create a safe and supportive place for the student to learn and engage in the research process. By providing this support, instructors can help students successfully collaborate and contribute meaningful research to their chosen fields.

References

Anderson, L., Bonds-Raacke, J., & Raacke, J. (2015). Looking to succeed?Understanding the importance of research publications. Retrieved from http://www.apa.org/ed/precollege/psn/2015/01/research-publications.aspx

CUR- The Council on Undergraduate Research (2011). Retrieved from https://www.cur.org/about_cur/fact_sheet/

Norcross, J. C. (2014, January). Getting involved in research as an undergraduate: Nuts and bolts. Retrieved from http://www.apa.org/ed/precollege/psn/2014/01/research-undergraduate.aspx.

Catherine Burke, Spalding University
Autumn Truss, Spalding University
DeDe Wohlfarth, Spalding University

VI. Diversity/Global Learning

The following are characteristics of this HIP:
- Students explore cultures outside their own, both at home and abroad.
- Emphasis is placed on differences, be they racial, ethnic, or gender.
- Often the students are involved in experiential learning, immersing themselves in another culture at home or abroad.

This section contains nine articles. Have you done a personal cultural inventory to understand your own culture before experiencing another? If your institution does not have a study abroad type experience available for students, why not?

A New Framework for 21st Century Classrooms

Historically, the word diversity commonly denoted differences between people, say minority Black Americans and White Americans. The word now has become expanded to include socio-economic status, age, physical abilities, religious beliefs, sexual orientation, political beliefs, and a host of other ideologies. In short, it has become the catch phrase for acknowledging, supporting, and protecting individual differences. Diversity is important as it fundamentally deals with how to respect one another despite our differences. Yet, it appears that while diversity acknowledges differences, it has had minimum impact on our basic human practices and behavior. Thus, while diversity is an important theme, this essay suggests that diversity as a high impact practice be reframed for the classroom to address four constructs, including (a) academic, (b) democratic, (c) moral and (d) economic. Let's briefly explore each of these four constructs.

Academic Construct

As we meander toward the end of the 21st century, we are faced with serious challenges to our current research models. Researchers are finally acknowledging that minorities are not well represented in clinical trials. In fact, Oh (2015) suggests that a lot of biomedical research not only does not reflect minorities, but it does not reflect the American population. He further states that "only 2 percent of cancer studies and less than 5 percent of pulmonary studies" have enough diversity to provide any generalizable information. One consequence of this phenomenon is that medications given to minority patients may not work or even cause greater problems.

University researchers should be intentional in creating more diverse participant study subjects in order to increase the accuracy and generalizability of the research study results. This construct is difficult because some minorities groups, say Black Americans, are very distrustful of most research studies as they have been historically targeted and exploited in the past—e.g., the Tuskegee Syphilis study. However, it is important that researchers not only be more diverse, but that research study participants be more reflective of the diversity that exists on college campuses and in the US. Diversity in research studies is important, and having more diverse instructors can be equally as important.

Many recent scholarly studies show that including diversity has many positive values, including improving performance, more accurate projections, and promoting creative thinking. In classrooms, having more diverse instructors creates a greater sense of belonging for minority students and allows for all students to benefit from different perspectives. In short, diversity in university research and in the classroom has several benefits--it can make us better people, yet homogeneity in research and teaching still dominates most research studies and college classooms.

Democratic Construct

Institutions of higher education should educate students to participate in a global democratic society. One way to accomplish this goal is to equip the students with the needed critical skills and capabilities that will allow them to critique, reflect, and recognize institutional and structural inequities. Thomas (2008) argues that students should become involved in social, cultural, and economic issues. Further, the democratic ideals of intergroup dialogue, democratic leadership, civic learning, and diversity must be fostered and valued in today's classrooms.

All students should have a firm grasp on democracy's guiding principles, which include equity, justice, and freedom for all. Students should be exposed to the economic systems that are exploitive, militaristic expeditions' specific targets, wealth distribution patterns that favor one group of persons over other groups, tax plans that generate great saving for certain groups, and how special interest groups impact government laws. Since the United States is becoming more pluralistic, it is prudent for classrooms to include more intergroup dialogue, reasoning, and discussion of the democratic ideals that founded this country. An important outcome, then, of higher education is to produce students who are able to understand how broader society works and have their own vision of how to become change agents in society for the betterment of all its citizenry. Banks (2008) argues that to be effective global citizens, all students should be active participants in society and socially aware. In fact, he suggests that it is a democratic imperative to educate our students along this democratic construct.

Moral Construct

Norman (2017) reports on a recent poll that showed Americans believe that moral values have been on a decline for over the past fifteen years. In fact, the poll suggested that 77% say that the state of moral values is getting worse. Further, in recent headlines during the latter part of 2017, we have been inundated with news reports highlighting improper sexual relationships between teachers and students as well as sexual harassment by college professors and persons in leadership positions across the board from college athletics to news anchors to entertainment moguls and politicians.

Further, people in leadership positions openly endorse positions that condone unfair and questionable practices. In the midst of this highly volatile environment, there must be a clarion call for truth and justice. Institutions of higher learning should refocus their curriculum to include an emphasis on character development and integrity. Educators can play an important role in this effort by having open dialogue with students. Thus, diversity efforts should include an emphasis on nurturing and supporting high moral standards for persons in leadership positions, especially for women and minorities who are often the victims of negative moral behavior.

Economic Construct

Jan (2017) reports that the despite the income and wealth gains of Black Americans and other minorities, the median net worth of them compared to White Americans remains a huge gap. In fact, for Black Americans, it is more than nine times the size. In 2014, all minority-owned businesses accounted for only 3.3% of employer receipts, while White American receipts accounted for the remaining 96.7 receipts (Alcorn, 2016). In the US, the nation's wealth has been increasingly concentrated in the communities of the richest Americans. This statistic suggests that for minority communities who are already behind, their incomes decreased or only showed minimum gain.

As our nation becomes more culturally and ethnically pluralistic, it is crucial that more economic opportunities be created. Institutions of higher learning should place greater emphasis on teaching students the value of economic independence. This process can range from workshops on the advantages/disadvantages of student loans, how to handle credit cards and the power of investing. Several advantages for increasing students' knowledge of economic principles include raising the standard of living, increasing our country's output, and helping our country develop. Higher education should consider it a curricular goal to make students more aware of the economics of obtaining a college degree.

Conclusion

In this essay I have attempted to broaden the role of diversity as a high impact practice to encompass a more global perspective that will benefit all of our students. The four constructs of diversity as discussed, if embraced, might lead to better relationships, more understanding, less hostility, and greater civility among our students as well as make them better prepared to be global citizens. This brief essay suggests that diversity when treated in this manner, focuses on an epistemological approach that will promote the best practices in human nature.

References

Alcorn, C. (2016). *Black businesses are on the rise in the U.S.* Retrieved from: http://www.fortune.com.

Banks, J. (2008). Teaching for social justice, diversity & citizenship in a global world. *Education Forum, 68(Summer),* 289-98.

Jan, T. (2017). *White families have nearly ten times the net worth of black families. And the gap is still growing.* Retrieved from https://www.washingtonpost.com/news/wonk/wp/2017/09/28/black-and-hispanic-families-are-making-more-money-but-they-still-lag-far-behind-whites/?utm_term=.503b138f4eb7.

Norman, J. (2017). *Views of U.S. moral values slip to seven-year lows.* Retrieved from http://www.news.gallup.com.

Oh, S. (2015). Lack of Diversity in Clinical Trials Presents Possible Health Consequences. Retrieved from https://www.npr.org/2015/12/15/459871070/lack-of-diversity-in-clinical-trials-presents-possible-health-consequences.

Thomas, N. (2008). Reframing and reclaiming democracy: Higher education's challenge. *Peer Review 10(2/3),* 9-12.

Timothy Forde, Eastern Kentucky University

A Passport to Innovation: Teaching Abroad

According to the National Survey of Student Engagement, study abroad is a high-impact practice that can be "life-changing." Teaching abroad can also be life-changing. As a faculty member, leading a study abroad class almost always requires shifting your pedagogical style to fit on-site resources, but it's an incredibly rewarding experience in professional development.

As with any new course prep, planning is vital. This list aims to help you in the adjustment process.

- **Location, Location, Location.** Because you'll need to design class materials and assignments based on the area, do some research about the city and its relevant sites for your class. The syllabus shouldn't look like it could be taught on your home campus.
- **Happy Campers.** Be prepared to serve in your usual identity as faculty member but also in a Student Life role. This adjustment includes being there for the students in ways you might not have performed before:

- Giving directions in a place you're learning along with them;
- Serving as a late-night sounding board about roommate problems;
- Soothing and distracting the students from homesickness;
- Reminding them that while other countries may have lower drinking ages, locals do not view drunkenness favorably; and
- Perhaps most importantly, accompanying students on the site school's cultural and extracurricular activities.

You don't need to spend 24/7 with them, but your students should know you are there for them, which definitely means arriving in the country earlier and leaving later than the students.

- **Your Host with the Most…Information.** Get to know your host school's faculty and staff. Regularly stop in at the main office of the school/department to say "Good morning" to the staff in their language, send your syllabus to the academic leader(s), hang out in the faculty lounge, and invite faculty peers out for coffee. In a short time, you'll develop friendships with folks around the world, and you will be more likely to receive an invitation to return.
- **Creature Comforts**. Adjust your expectations of American air conditioning, transportation, fast Internet, convenient laundry facilities, and other daily luxuries. When the professor complains about the loss of daily American privileges, such as the amount of walking or the lack of clothes dryers, it gives the students license to do the same and to pay more attention to problems than to the overall positive experience.
- **Stay Calm and Teach.** Teaching Abroad is not a vacation. It's work. Bringing family members along can be fun, but be sure to let them know that you are teaching what is probably a new prep in a highly concentrated term and may not be able to accompany them on sight-seeing adventures. Alternatively, you could add a week before or after the class term for a family vacation, but don't expect your university to foot the bill.
- **Don't Curb Your Enthusiasm.** Chances are that you are excited to teach abroad and in the location of your choice, far away from your campus community. If you're happy about being across the world with a group of students who probably haven't been there before, show it! Your enthusiasm is contagious, wherever you are.

Teaching Abroad can be one of the most fulfilling experiences of your teaching career, and you'll surely be more innovative in your teaching style as you adapt to the resources available to you at the site. Plus, you can be certain that you will lead your students toward a life-changing experience.

Lisa Day, Eastern Kentucky University
Jennifer White, Eastern Kentucky University

Making Immersion Experiences During Multicultural Training Appropriate and Meaningful for Minority Students

Cultural competence is considered an integral component of many educational curricula and encompasses "the awareness, knowledge, and skills needed to function effectively with culturally diverse populations" (Sue & Sue, 2016, p. 747). While knowledge acquisition through reading and class discussions may form the basis of multicultural training, students are frequently encouraged or required to engage in real-world immersion experiences. These projects typically involve students leaving the classroom to have direct contact with individuals with whom they have little familiarity and may actually be biased toward. Immersion experiences help students put into practice knowledge they acquired in class, gain a greater appreciation for the barriers individuals from a particular group face, and challenge their beliefs about said group (Hevia, 2012).

Despite immersion experiences being a core component of higher educational learning, seemingly little attention has been paid to the unique challenges of students with marginalized or minority identities when completing such assignments. Even the basic guidelines for selecting an immersion experience can reflect this bias. For instance, some instructors require that the target group (i.e., the group a student plans to spend time with) be marginalized or face discrimination (Hevia, 2012). This choice can be an easy task for some students who do not routinely face discrimination (e.g., White cisgender men). By comparison, students with marginalized identities inherently have fewer groups to select, as they represent a target group, thereby making the assignment more burdensome. For example, where is a LGBTQ African-American female student to complete her immersion experience? Additionally, given that belonging to a minority group does not prevent someone from having biases against another minority group, the immersion experiences may place marginalized students at risk for discrimination, or even violence, by those in the target group while completing the assignment.

A lack of consideration for how marginalized students navigate challenges related to immersion experiences appears to mirror common critiques from some students of color in graduate counseling programs who report that their multicultural courses seem primarily designed for White students (Seward, 2014). Indeed, some quantitative research appears to validate such concerns, as evidence suggests receiving multicultural training only enhances White students' levels of multicultural awareness but does not equally contribute to the training of their racial/ethnic minority peers (Chao, Wei, Good, Flores, 2011). Unfortunately, given the dearth of research regarding marginalized students and immersion experiences, instructors may be unsure how to best proceed with structuring guidelines for these assignments in support of all students. In light of this situation, we suggest the following recommendations as a starting point when considering having students complete immersion experiences.

1. Allow students to design their own type of immersion experience, rather than forcing them to pick from a pre-determined set of categories (e.g., race, sexual orientation, etc.) or particular locations/organizations (e.g., a local homeless shelter). This flexibility allows students to self-reflect and then choose an experience that will enhance their multicultural knowledge (Pope-Davis, Breaux, & Liu, 1997). Self-reflection before the immersion experience also allows students to anticipate challenges of the assignment. Given that students with marginalized identities may risk discrimination as they complete their assignments, professors should meet individually with students to help ensure they remain safe during the assignment. Based on students' self-reflections, instructors and students can work together to make plans to address any concerns about a chosen immersion experience (e.g., creating a safety plan).

2. When an appropriate immersion experience does not appear to exist for a student, or if identified safety concerns are unable to be adequately addressed, instructors should provide an alternate assignment. Care should be taken so that the assignment does not further stigmatize the student or contribute to additional experiences of marginalization. Appropriate alternate assignments might include reflection papers on the student's experience of belonging to a marginalized group and the resulting impact on their identity development. Research has also suggested that the use of film can positively impact multicultural knowledge (Greene, Barden, Richardson, & Hall, 2014). Film selections should serve to challenge stereotypes or confront clashing cultural iden-

tities. The films selected should evoke emotion and thought in students, and instructors should lead discussions with students after they have viewed the film (Greene et al., 2014). The overall guiding principle should be choosing assignments that are beneficial to students' multicultural training and personal growth.
3. Offer students multiple opportunities to debrief and process their experiences. These chances to debrief may be accomplished in individual meetings, in a larger classroom setting, or within smaller groups of students. Instructors may also be proactive and reach out to students to initiate the debriefing process, as some students may be hesitant to initiate such a conversation (Hipolito-Delgado, Estrada, & Garcia, 2017). Greene and colleagues (2014) found that creating a collaborative dialogue after having students engage in experiential learning activities led to greater understanding and appreciation of others' worldviews and experiences. If these dialogues occur during class, instructors must ensure that conversations remain respectful and genuine for all students involved, and facilitate a space that is safe for students to share honestly.

In sum, when implementing immersion experiences to enhance multicultural awareness in the educational setting, instructors need to carefully consider the perspective of and impact on minority students. Instructors should allow students to pick an immersion experience that is appropriate for them, offer alternative assignments when needed, and provide multiple opportunities to debrief. The ultimate goal is to ensure that all students benefit from immersion experiences and continue their journeys toward enhancing and applying their multicultural knowledge beyond the classroom.

References

Chao, R., Wei, M., Good, G., & Flores, L. (2011). Race/ethnicity, color-blind racial attitudes, and multicultural counseling competence: The moderating effects of multicultural counseling training. *Journal of Counseling Psychology, 58*(1), 72-82.

Greene, J. H., Barden, S. M., Richardson, E. D., & Hall, K. G. (2014). The influence of film and experiential pedagogy on multicultural counseling self-efficacy and multicultural counseling competence. *Journal of the Scholarship of Teaching and Learning, 14*(5), 63-78.

Hevia, J. M. (2012). Experience is the best teacher: Designing immersion projects for multicultural education. *International Journal of University Teaching and Faculty Development, 3*(1), 59-68.

Pope-Davis, D. B., Breaux, C., & Liu, W. M. (1997). A multicultural immersion experience: Filling a void in multicultural training. In D. B. Pope-Davis & H. L. K. Coleman (Eds.), *Multicultural counseling competencies: Assessment, education and training, and supervision* (pp. 227-241). Thousand Oaks, CA: Sage Publications.

Hipolito-Delgado, C. P., Estrada, D., & Garcia, M. (2017). Diversifying counsellor education: A case study of U.S. students of colour. *British Journal of Guidance & Counseling, 45*(5), 473-488.

Seward, D. (2014). Multicultural course pedagogy: Experiences of master's-level students of color. *Counselor Education & Supervision, 53*, 62-79.

Sue, D. W., & Sue, D. (2016). *Counseling the culturally diverse: Theory and practice* (7th ed.). Hoboken, NJ: Wiley & Sons, Inc.

David W. Hutsell, Spalding University
Nardin A. Michaels, Spalding University
Lauren Holder, Spalding University
DeDe Wohlfarth, Spalding University

What Makes a Good Study Abroad Program?

"Travel is fatal to prejudice, bigotry, and narrow-mindedness, and many of our people need it sorely on these accounts. Broad, wholesome, charitable views of men and things cannot be acquired by vegetating in one little corner of the earth all one's lifetime." –Mark Twain

According to The Institute of International Education, 304,467 students studied abroad in the 2013-2014 school year, a number that has tripled over the last twenty years (Smith & Mrozek, 2016). Although the absolute number of college students studying abroad has increased, the percentage of students who take advantage of this opportunity has remained constant (Salisbury, 2012). This essay will provide a brief overview of the benefits and barriers to study abroad programs.

Benefits to Studying Abroad

Intercultural development. Intercultural awareness develops as students experience, understand, and adapt to cultures different from their own. While study abroad programs clearly foster learning about other cultures, they also promote understanding of the students' cultures through inevitable comparisons. This comparison can deepen students' understanding of their own cultural and national identities (Bandyopadhyay & Bandyopadhyay, 2015).

Personal growth and development. Studying abroad gives students the opportunity to discover themselves. Being by oneself in a new place can be overwhelming at times, but can also encourage students' problem-solving skills and ability to adjust to new situations (Bandyopadhyay & Bandyopadhyay, 2015).

Professional development. Students grow as professionals through travel abroad by narrowing their career choices or reconsidering them all together. These experiences also help students to imagine how their career might be practiced in another culture and strengthen the cultural skills necessary to succeed at their chosen career in their home countries (Bandyopadhyay & Bandyopadhyay, 2015).

Barriers to Studying Abroad

Colleges and universities may unintentionally create obstacles that can often discourage students from studying abroad, including these common barriers:

1. High Cost (Williamson, 2010)
2. Academic expectations that do not accommodate study abroad experiences (Williamson, 2010)
3. Lack of fostering the experience by university staff (Williamson, 2010)
4. Lack of resources (Smith & Mrozek, 2012)
5. Social anxiety about going without one's friends (Smith & Mrozek, 2012)
6. Intercultural communication apprehension, or the normal anxiety related to interactions with individuals of other cultures (Bandyopadhyay & Bandyopadhyay, 2015)

How Can We Make This Situation Better?

To surmount these barriers, the following recommendations may be helpful to make study abroad programs more accessible:

Support from faculty and staff. The university's faculty and administrators need to work together to support study abroad experiences. Administrators have the power to finance, but professors and other staff members have the power to influence students by promoting study abroad experiences (Williamson, 2010). Students need to know that study abroad programs are relevant to their major field. Students in the social sciences and humanities fields more easily recognize the relevance of study abroad trips than those in the physical sciences and pre-professional programs, thus extra effort may be needed to reach all students (Bandyopadhyay & Bandyopadhyay, 2015).

Simplicity of application process. Successful study abroad programs make the application process as simple as possible. This facilitation might involve assisting in obtaining visas or passports, making flight arrangements, and providing travel tips (Bandyopadhyay & Bandyopadhyay, 2015).

Promotion of the benefits of study abroad. If students clearly understand the benefits of studying abroad, they will be more likely to participate. Students should understand that study abroad can increase self-reliance, focus their career goals, develop their proficiency of a foreign language, and aid in their academic performance. Faculty and parents play critical roles in encouraging study abroad trips (Bandyopadhyay & Bandyopadhyay, 2015).

Numerous program options. Historically, study abroad programs have offered limited financial aid, few course equivalencies, and little academic credit. Successful study abroad initiatives offer an array of programs supported by multiple academic departments. Good study abroad experiences also provide flexibility so students can individualize their experiences (Williamson, 2010). For example, The University of Minnesota-Twin Cities has developed "study abroad major advising sheets" that other universities have adopted to assist in academic planning. These sheets allow students, advisers, professors, and study abroad professionals to match students' interest in varying academic programs with study abroad programs. This approach views the study abroad experience as an embedded educational experience rather than a superfluous extracurricular one (Bandyopadhyay & Bandyopadhyay, 2015).

Risk preparation. Successful study abroad programs help students prepare for a successful trip, including working with judicial affairs, health services, disability services, and the counseling center. Vital training also includes health and safety of students, health insurance, crisis-management protocols, and tips for international living (Williamson, 2010).

Fair Price. Study-abroad programs are often not cheap, nor are they necessarily nonprofit. However, successful study abroad programs are transparent about finances (Williamson, 2010). A key factor in study abroad programs is affordability as students often choose not to study abroad due to financial constraints. Offering financial aid or scholarships reduces the financial burden and allows more students to study abroad (Bandyopadhyay & Bandyopadhyay, 2015).

Students earn credit towards graduation. Successful study abroad programs consider the students' career paths when allowing students to earn credit towards their major, minor, or general education requirements. The "study" in study abroad is vital. Students should consider their study abroad classes as part of their overall education toward their career goal (Williamson, 2010).

References

Bandyopadhyay, S. & Bandyopadhyay, K (2015). Factors influencing student participation in college study abroad programs. *Journal of International Education Research, 11*(2), 87-94.

Salisbury, M. (2012). We're muddying the message on Study Abroad. *The Chronicle of Higher Education.* Retrieved from http://www.chronicle.com/article/Were-Muddying-the-Message-on/133211.

Smith, P. J. & Mrozek, L. J. (2016). Evaluating the application of program outcomes to study abroad experiences. *Honors in Practice, 12*, 9-32.

Williamson, W. (2010). 7 signs of successful study-abroad programs. *The Chronicle of Higher Education.* Retrieved from http://www.chronicle.com/article/7-Signs-of-Successful/123657.

Sabrina Kordes, Spalding University

HIP HIP Here and Away

In recent years, educators have identified key practices that have shown success in student retention and preparation for professional endeavors. In many ways, these practices coined as high impact (HIP) are descriptive of the kind of experiences students have as foreign language students, particularly through diversity and global learning. These concepts shape curricula and programming to make students successful at home and away. These days, one hears that everything is global, but the local culture and linguistic practices cannot be ignored. It seems, then, that HIPs are not only effective for students, but they help us see how we fit in the global picture. The focus of higher education is shifting, and one can only hope the information on what works to prepare students will not be forgotten or eliminated.

With the changing landscape of public education, one sometimes must wonder just what happened to the American promise to educate citizens to be well-rounded critical thinkers; not to mention the literature on teaching and learning regarding what leads to student success. The American Association of Colleges and Universities (AACU) in their projects affiliated with Liberal Education and America's Promise (LEAP); and more recently, with Indiana University's Valid Assessment of Learning in Undergraduate Education (VALUE) Institute, have validated the importance of high-impact educational practices on student retention and success. Since so much of what makes up these HIPs is related to collaboration and community-centered learning, we must continue to offer (and fund) courses, experiences, and endeavors that are undeniably high impact. Content knowledge is key to success, but cannot be the sole formation developed for students today. Neglecting to provide students ample exposure to HIPs is denying them the American education promise.

As a foreign language professor, I can say that HIPs are built into the programs we offer students, and in many ways make up the core of our student learning goals and outcomes. By creating communities of learners that are open and inclusive, many of the HIPs are met or become attainable practices. Here, I will highlight diversity and global learning and how we can use service and community-based learning to create *glocal* learning. The term *glocal* (and *glocalization*) is an extension of globalization and global and describes an environment where products and services are most successful when they are customized for the local consumers. To create and market products, services, and communication in global networks requires linguistic and cultural competence. For this reason, the National Education Society has declared global competence a 21st- Century Imperative. Global competence refers to the acquisition of " in-depth knowledge and understanding of international issues, an appreciation of and ability to learn and work with people from diverse linguistic and cultural backgrounds, proficiency in a foreign language, and skills to function productively in an interdependent world community" (NES). The foreign language classroom and the activities and communities that surround it strive to take knowledge of diversity and global issues and mix them with local ones to create mutual understanding. Foreign language curricula often include many of the HIP from common intellectual experiences to learning communities, diversity and global learning, service learning, community-based learning, and internships.

The scaffolding of known to unknown variables that are addressed in language classes provides students with the linguistic and cultural competence to engage globally for study abroad, international internships, or work study/ co-op programs with international companies. Through language, cultural clues are discovered and open the door for a more profound understanding of *glocalization*. The various endeavors of foreign language teachers, study abroad, and international advisors as well as others are fruitful for effective community-based learning in a variety of settings. Some of these efforts are described in a recent volume edited by Melanie Bloom and Carolyn Gascoigne about creating and implementing learning opportunities for language learners. *Creating Experiential Learning Opportunities for Language Learners* (2017) is a great guide and inspiration to anyone seeking more ways to create communities here and abroad.

Those looking to implement more HIPs on campus and in their classes and programs should consider one or more of the following activities.
1. Recruit international students and help them to collaborate with domestic students.
2. Invite guest speakers from a variety of backgrounds.
3. Offer ample service learning opportunities that expose students to unknown groups and cultures.
4. Develop relationships with local businesses with international partners.
5. Develop relationships with service providers such as hospitals, local libraries, and K-12 schools.
6. Host internationally focused events.
7. Encourage study abroad and appropriate preparation for it.

8. Show students how they can collect data of their engagement through ePortfolios (one of the newest HIPs).
9. Encourage students to seek credit for prior learning when applicable.
10. Encourage students to think, learn and live globally and *glocally*.

This list is far from exhaustive, so using creativity and thinking outside the box are key. As educators aim to further integrate HIPs into the learning process, we must keep in mind that knowledge allows the pathway to mutual understanding that can break down barriers. Thus, let us continue to cultivate global awareness that will lead to citizens who think and act globally and *glocally*. This strategy will allow us to form communities through HIPs both here and away. *Bon voyage*!

References

Bloom, M., & Carolyn G. (eds) (2017). *Creating experiential learning opportunities for language learners*. Multilingual Matters.

Kuh, G. (2008). *High-Impact educational practices, what they are, who has access to them, and why they matter.* (2008). AACU. Retrieved from https://keycenter.unca.edu/sites/default/files/aacu_high_impact_2008_final.pdf

NEA Education Policy and Practice Department (2010). *Global competence Is a 21st century imperative*. Retrieved from http://www.nea.org/assets/docs/HE/PB28A_Global_Competence11.pdf

Randi L. Polk, Eastern Kentucky University

Creating Culturally Responsive Classrooms

Many educators dichotomize the concepts of culture and learning. As such, we write this essay to address these two statements:

1. It is not my job to teach cultural diversity. I teach chemistry. Cultural issues are not relevant.
2. Evidence-based teaching is sufficiently good teaching. If I teach consistent with best practices, then I will be reaching all students, including students of color.

The goal of this essay is to challenge these views by providing data that supports how diversity is inextricably connected with culture. We also will share ideas to create more culturally responsive classrooms.

How Are Culture and Learning Connected?

1. Society is not just. Instead, it privileges some and oppresses others. This oppression can be seen in racism, sexism and heterosexism, which have been codified into our society's laws and infrastructure. If all people had equal access to resources, then the percentages of minorities, women, and LGBTQ people in our professions would mirror society. Yet only 6% of computer programmers are black and only 3% of chemists are Hispanic (Heylin, 2007; Lee & Mather, 2008). In contrast, our society is 13% black and 18% Hispanic (U.S. Census Bureau, 2017).
2. Students of color and poor students are disproportionally educated in weak schools. White and upper socio-economic students have greater access to laboratories, dual credit classes and, most significantly, better teachers with more teaching experience and higher teaching evaluations. Lower SES schools are more likely to focus on discipline than academics (Wilson, Hugenberg & Rule, 2017). Children of color are also more likely to be placed in special education classes, less likely to be placed in gifted programs, and receive harsher discipline for the same behavior as white students (Wilson, Hugenberg & Rule, 2017; Rudd, 2014). Although these statements are generalizations, to ignore these facts is problematic because we assume that every student has similar access to opportunities.
3. Students of color are not provided equal access to higher education. Although college acceptance rates among students of color have increased, the overall number of students of color accepted at universities is still dismal (Snyder, de Brey & Dillow, 2016), reflecting a gate-keeping mechanism that welcomes some but not others. Professors and employers tend to create more opportunities for individuals who are male and have white-sounding names than those who are females and with ethnic-sounding names (Fryer & Levitt, 2003; King, Mendoza, Madera, Hebl & Knight, 2006).
4. Current teaching tends to reinforce existing societal structures that privilege some and marginalize others. Our goal should be to teach critical pedagogy—

to encourage students to question existing societal structures and be empowered to improve them.
5. Course textbooks and the content we teach, even the examples we give in our classrooms, are likely to reflect male, white, Christian, and straight perspectives. History classes are teeming with such examples, but examples abound in every subject. Many of us struggle to see this veil of whiteness because we often share this world view; in fact, 84% of full-time professors identify as non-minority (Sue, 2016).
6. Our classrooms typically reflect a style of communication that tends to be low-context dependent, heavily verbal, devalue silence, and less passionate and expressive than high-context communication (Sue & Sue, 2016). Many cultures, including Hispanic, black, Asian, and Native American, are high context communicators, and focus more on nonverbal cues of the message than words themselves (Sue & Sue, 2016). Students of color may thus feel marginalized, disengaged, or disadvantaged in some classes.
7. Our students of color and LGBTQ students lack role models. As of 2015, only 16% of full-time college professors were minorities. This lack of role models leads to an increase in imposter syndrome among marginalized students, who may feel as if they "don't belong" in academia, and were admitted by mistake. While imposter syndrome is common among all students, marginalized students are especially likely to experience it (Cokley, McClain, Enciso & Martinez, 2013).
8. Microaggressions are common in classrooms. 65% of students of color report regularly experiencing microaggressions (unintentional slights and hostility directed at marginalized people) in their classrooms (Boysen, 2012). These microaggressions are perpetuated equally by classmates and professors. Those who espouse a "colorblind" perspective are particularly likely to commit microaggressions (Offermann, Basford, Graebner, Jaffer, De Graaf & Kaminsky, 2014). Sadly, 44% of students of color experience outright racism on their college campuses (Boysen, 2012).

How Can We Create More Culturally Responsive Classrooms?

1. Admit that you may have unintentionally inherited some racist, sexist and heterosexist views from our society. Self-reflect on how your biases affect your teaching.

2. When you commit microaggressions in your classrooms or relationships, apologize. Seek feedback from others, especially those in disempowered groups, and learn it. Ask your students to let you know if/when you commit a microaggression.
3. Call out and stop microaggressions when they happen in your class, including the myth of colorblindness. A statement on the first day of class can help, like: "I will point out microaggressions when they happen in our class. It might make people a little uncomfortable, but we will all learn from it."
4. When you hear a racist, sexist, or heterosexist joke, make it awkward for the person telling the joke by asking why that person thinks the joke is funny.
5. Build real relationships with all people who are different from you, not just students of color. When a white professor interacts with a student of color, the power differential between the two maintains society's existing power structure. Seeking out others different from you—especially in egalitarian relationships—helps decrease biases (Zebrowitz, White & Wieneke, 2008).
6. Openly talk to students about the imposter syndrome.
7. Be an active, involved advisor. When educators reach out early, often, and intentionally, student outcomes are likely to be more positive (Toldson, Braithwaite, & Rentie, 2009; Umbach & Wawrzynski, 2005).
8. Use culturally relevant examples and names. Create a classroom that honors and celebrates students' backgrounds and lived experiences instead of ignoring them or devaluing them.

References

Boysen, G. A. (2012). Teacher and student perceptions of microaggressions in college classrooms. *College Teaching, 60,* 122-129. doi: 10.1080/87567555.2012.654831.

Cokley, K., McClain, S., Enciso, A., & Martinez, M. (2013). An examination of the impact of minority status stress and impostor feelings on the mental health of diverse ethnic minority college students. *Journal of Multicultural Counseling and Development, 41(2),* 82-95.

Fryer, R. G., & Levitt, S. D. (2003). *The causes and consequences of distinctively black names* (No. w9938). National Bureau of Economic Research.

Heylin, M. (2007). ACS News. Retrieved March 11, 2017, from http://pubs.acs.org/cen/email/html/cen_85_i38_8538acsnews.html

King, E. B., Mendoza, S. A., Madera, J. M., Hebl, M. R., & Knight, J. L. (2006). What's in a name? A multiracial investigation of the role of occupational stereotypes in selection decisions. *Journal of Applied Social Psychology, 36(5),* 1145-1159.

Lee, M., & Mather, M. (2008). *US labor force trends* (Vol. 63, No. 2). Population Reference Bureau.

McFarland, J., Hussar, B., de Brey, C., Snyder, T., Wang, X., Wilkinson-Flicker, S., ... & Bullock Mann, F. (2017). The Condition of Education 2017. NCES 2017-144. *National Center for Education Statistics*.

Offermann, L. R., Basford, T. E., Graebner, R., Jaffer, S., De Graaf, S. B., & Kaminsky, S. E. (2014). See no evil: Color blindness and perceptions of subtle racial discrimination in the workplace. *Cultural Diversity and Ethnic Minority Psychology, 20*(4), 499.

Snyder, T. D., de Brey, C., & Dillow, S. A. (2016). Digest of Education Statistics 2014, NCES 2016-006. *National Center for Education Statistics*.

Sue, D. W., & Sue, D. (2016). *Counseling the culturally diverse: Theory and practice.* Hoboken, NJ: John Wiley.

Sue, D. W. (2017). Microaggressions and "evidence": Empirical or experiential reality? *Perspectives on Psychological Science, 12*(1), 170-172.

Rudd, T. (2014). Racial disproportionality in school discipline: Implicit bias is heavily implicated. *Kirwan Institute for the Study of Race and Ethnicity*. Retrieved from: http://kirwaninstitute.osu.edu/wp-content/uploads/2014/02/racial-disproportionalityschools-02.pdf.

Toldson, I. A., Braithwaite, R. L., & Rentie, R. J. (2009). Promoting college aspirations among school-age Black American males. In *Black American males in higher education: Research, programs and academe* (pp. 117-137). Emerald Group Publishing Limited.

Umbach, P. D., & Wawrzynski, M. R. (2005). Faculty do matter: The role of college faculty in student learning and engagement. *Research in Higher Education, 46*(2), 153-184.

Wilson, J. P., Hugenberg, K., & Rule, N. O. (2017). Racial bias in judgments of physical size and formidability: From size to threat. *Journal of Personality and Social Psychology*. Advance online publication.

U.S. Census Bureau. Quick Facts. https://www.census.gov/quickfacts/fact/table/US/PST045216

Zebrowitz, L. A., White, B., & Wieneke, K. (2008). Mere exposure and racial prejudice: Exposure to other-race faces increases liking for strangers of that race. *Social cognition, 26*(3), 259-275.

Truman Harris, M.S., Spalding University
Mistalene Calleroz White, Spalding University
Jacqueline McMillan-Bohler, Spalding University
DeDe Wohlfarth, Spalding University

Can 100 People Tell a Meaningful Story?

Diversity/Global Learning

Thomas Friedman, in his book *The World is Flat*, explains that the changes occurring in our world today create a dynamic and fluid world. As future teachers and leaders in local communities, individuals must be equipped with tools to view what is happening in their community, as well as what occurs globally, with a critical eye. The goal of this essay is to initiate the conversation about how we, as educators, support what it means to be a global society and what responsibilities we hold as members.

Hicks (2001) theorizes that in order for a strong economic and stable society to be built, five areas need to be central to education so that young students see their world critically:

1. we live in a world of rapid change where yesterday's certainties are no longer an effective guide to tomorrow;
2. developing foresight, the ability to think ahead more clearly and thoughtfully, is increasingly a vital survival skill;
3. we need to be more aware of the range of alternative futures, possible, probable and preferable, that may be open to us;
4. we need to think more carefully about how choices in the present will have consequences for both people and planet in future time; and
5. this should help us to make wiser choices in the present, leading to a more responsible and future-orientated citizenship (pg. 231).

Students' ability to look critically and creatively at those areas that influence their world will provide necessary skills that will, and must, be utilized for a lifetime.

Skovsmose (2011) discussed the notion of landscapes of investigation. Unlike the traditional curriculum seen in schools, landscapes of investigation allow students to approach unfamiliar topics and construct meaningful knowledge as they engage in and discover new information. One vital component of such investigations is understanding that while students cannot be forced into action, instructors must disturb the current funds of knowledge that they hold regarding a specific topic.

Students come into our classes carrying a set of beliefs. Implementing a landscape of investigation does not claim to change an individual's belief system, but encourages an individual to think more broadly about topics of which they may only have a superficial understanding. Information is often stripped down to depict only certain subjective viewpoints; therefore, when one seeks to provide the opportunity to look more holistically at a subject area, finding an objective vehicle becomes critical. In this case, mathematics will be used as the conduit between fact and perception.

A meaningful, non-threatening task to begin a conversation in regards to fact and perception is asking the question, "What would our world look like if it had only 100 people?" The task, as presented, was created and vetted in a course that takes ideas related to social justices and uses the lens of mathematics to support the foundations of quantitative literacy.

Task: For the initial work on this investigation, using only 100 people, estimate the characteristics listed below. Individuals can be placed in multiple sections; therefore, a total of 100 for each category must be attained.

Estimate the following:

If the world were 100 people, how many would be(have):
- Male/Female
- Age
- Religion (Christian, Muslim, Hindus, Buddhists, Other, No religion)
- Literacy/Non-literate
- College graduate
- Access to the Internet
- Access to telephones
- Clean Water
- Poverty
- Proper nutrition
- Housing
- Language (Chinese, Spanish, English, Hindi, Arabic, Portuguese, Russian, Japanese, German, Other)
- Live in Urban/Rural areas
- Live on each continent (North America, South America, Asia, Africa, Antarctica, Europe, Australia)

Gender	Female	Male	

Age	Children	Adults	Adults +65

Shared Tips for Effective Teaching / 109

Religion	Buddhist	Christians	Hindus	Muslim	Other	No Religion

Figure 1: Sample of Recording Tables

Once the students have completed their estimates, the infographic "The World as 100 People" is shared (see Figure 2). During this time, students are simply viewing and comparing current statistics with their perceived ideas related to worldwide population.

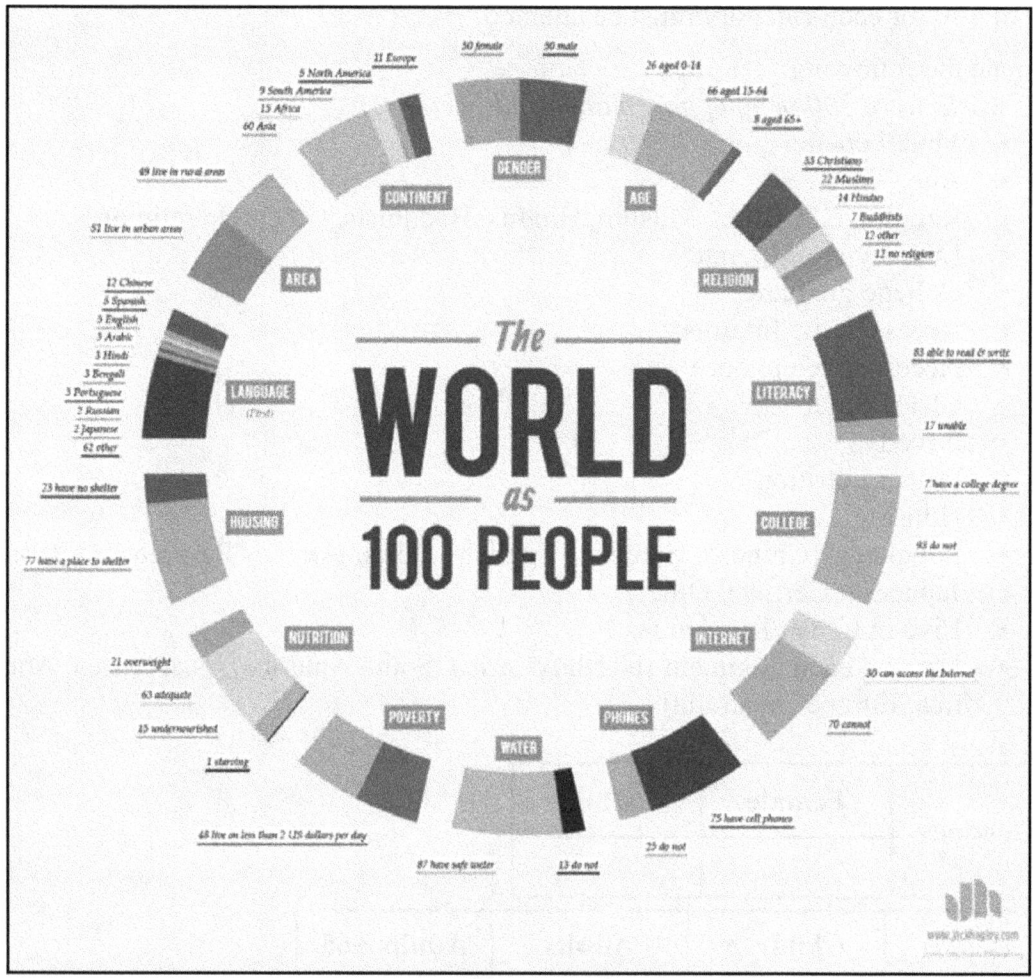

Figure 2: Infographic of the World as 100 People.
http://jackhagley.com/The-World-as-100-People

Once students have time to synthesize the information presented, the following prompts are displayed, and students are encouraged to discuss their concerns.

What do we SEE...
Reflecting on our noticing about:
- *Individual categories*
- *Labels within category*
- *Quantities in the infographic and/or in our predictions*
- *Provided definitions and/or data sources*
- *What do we THINK...*
- *What do you find most surprising from this information, and WHY is this surprising to you?*
- *In your own predictions, what were you accurate on (or not), and WHY do you think that you were (or not)?*
- *How do you make sense of the information and provided documents?*
- *What do we WONDER...*
- *What are you still wondering about related to global issues/information and WHY does this matter to you?*
- *Why might someone create this image? What are potential stories?*

After students have reconciled the information presented in the early part of the activity, the next section asks them to consider what they believe to be ten issues of global concern. This task can be done independently or within a group. According to 100 People: A World Portrait (http://100people.org/onehundred_lens_detail.php?subject=Water&section=100people#a), the ten areas of global concern are: water, food, transportation, health, economy, education, energy, shelter, wars, and waste. Once the class has discussed the ten areas of concern identified by the 100 People site, break the students up into groups and assign one of the videos found under Global Issues on the 100 People: A World Portrait website. During viewing the video, students should record three facts that they found interesting related to their topic. At the conclusion of the video, have the students share their facts and facilitate a class discussion based upon what the students present. Self-reflection becomes essential to the success of this assignment. At the conclusion of the lesson, ask the students to construct a written response that attends to the following prompts: Why is the issue of (their choice from the ten presented) important to me? What experience(s) have I faced in my life related to this issue? How might this issue be of critical importance to other people in the world who are different than me? Explain.

One of the main goals of implementing a task such as this is not to force an idea upon a student but, instead, to allow them to begin to see the world through a different lens. For many, this may be unchartered territory and may seem arduous, but with the correct supports in place, students can, and will, construct meaningful dialogue that allows for growth and change.

References

Friedman, T. (2005). *The world is flat: A brief history of the twenty-first century.* New York: Farrar, Straus, and Giroux.

Hicks, D. (2001). Re-examining the future: The challenge for citizenship education. *Educational Review, 53,* 229-240.

Skovsmose, O. (2011). *An invitation to critical mathematics education.* Rotterdam, Netherlands: Sense Publishers.

Lisa Poling, Appalachian State University
Tracy Goodson-Espy, Appalachian State University
Chrystal Dean, Appalachian State University

Discovering the Use of Interactive Scenarios to Address Diversity/Global Learning

Providing students with diverse experiences can be challenging. Experiential learning within a community is not always a viable option. Interactive scenarios can help students explore cultures, life experiences, and worldviews different from their own. Interactive scenarios allow the course content to be applied within a real-world context. The learner collects information, accesses it, and makes appropriate decisions, thus creating a more meaningful experience that impacts learning and assists the instructor in assessing the learner's understanding.

Interactive scenarios include the following three elements (Kuhlmann, 2009):

- **Challenge**: The goal is to engage the learner and challenge understanding. Present a situation, allow time to process the information, reflect, and then make a decision.
- **Choices**: Once the learner is challenged, she needs to make a decision (or series of decisions). Provide viable and realistic choices to work through the challenge.
- **Consequences**: Each choice produces a consequence. Sometimes the consequence leads to immediate feedback; sometimes it leads to additional challenges that compound the situation.

Software is available to create interactive scenarios; however, the cost may be prohibitive. Individuals can construct interactive scenarios in PowerPoint using the hyperlink option to link to other pages or use Google forms, which has a similar feature. Scenarios need not be overly complicated, should avoid descriptive writing, and can begin by jumping into the scenario.

I created an interactive scenario around a teacher who had a student with LGBTQ parents. Undergraduate students were asked to view the situation from the teacher's perspective and make a series of choices regarding what to do when confronted with moral and ethical dilemmas. Students had to work through the scenario and could not move onto the next page until a choice was made about a particular dilemma. With each choice the student made, a consequence and an additional challenge were presented, thus prompting the student to make another choice. At the end of the simulation, the undergraduate student was asked by the fictitious principal to create a professional development presentation regarding working with LGBTQ families. In an informal poll, the students reported enjoying working through the simulation. Several students reported working through the simulation several times making different choices each time. This assignment allowed students to explore "difficult differences" virtually through each choice they made and the provided consequence.

In a graduate level course, students were assigned to create a scenario. In order to create an interactive scenario, one must be very familiar with the content. I provided students with several resources to gain an understanding of interactive scenarios. They were asked to explore a provided website with several interactive scenarios. I also provided students with links to blogs and video tutorials on creating interactive scenarios.

Students began brainstorming topics and obtaining feedback from peers. Next, they were prompted to think through content and flow of a scenario using a hypothetical scenario:

Challenge: You suspect your best friend is in an abusive relationship.

What **Choices** do you have? 1) Ignore the issue 2) Confront your friend 3) Discuss with another friend

What are the **Consequences** based on your choice?

1) Ignoring the issue leads to.....your friend being seriously hurt (consequence)......new challenge (#2).....new choices (#2)...new consequences (#2)....new challenge (#3).....new choices (#3)...new consequences (#3)........ end with available resources (national hotlines, weblinks, pdfs, etc.) pertaining to intimate partner violence/dating violence/domestic violence.
2) Confronting your friend leads to....her telling you that she is being abused (consequence).....new challenge (#2).....new choices (#2)...new consequences (#2)....new challenge (#3).....new choices (#3)...new consequences (#3)........end with available resources (national hotlines, weblinks, pdfs, etc.) pertaining to intimate partner violence/dating violence/domestic violence.
3) Discussing this with a mutual friend leads to...the mutual friend confronting the friend you have concerns about (consequence)......new challenge (#2).....new choices (#2)...new consequences (#2)....new challenge (#3)..... new choices (#3)...new consequences (#3)........end with available resources (national hotlines, weblinks, pdfs, etc.) pertaining to intimate partner violence/dating violence/domestic violence.

Students then mapped out the scenario flow. Maps could be hand drawn or created within a computer program using a flowchart or mind mapping software (e.g., MindManager). Students were asked to post their map on the course discussion board and provide feedback to one another.

Last, students were instructed to create slides with content and a creative layout design. For the purposes of our class, the interactive scenario had to lead the learner to resources (national hotlines, weblinks, pdfs, infographics, etc.) pertaining to the chosen topic.

In conclusion, using interactive scenarios can engage learners in applying course content to real life situations within diverse contexts. In the area of social sciences, sometimes it is difficult to obtain experiences within a real world setting due to the sensitive nature of the topics and confidentiality. Using interactive scenarios provides a "safe way" for the student to make choices and discover consequences. It also allows me to assess the student's understanding of the application of the content. In my experience, interactive scenarios assist students with understanding the content and how working with individuals and families is difficult given the variety of choices and consequences.

To deepen a student's exploration of "difficult differences," interactive scenarios are helpful in developing an understanding of why individuals or families may be making certain choices. Asking students to create an interactive scenario allows them an opportunity to delve deeper into the content and engage in critical thinking as they design the sequence of the scenario.

Resources

Sample interactive scenarios:
   http://preventingbullying.promoteprevent.org/cyberbullying/interactive-scenarios

Creating interactive scenarios (branched scenarios) with PowerPoint:
   Interactive Scenario with PowerPoint (Long, in-depth video)
      https://www.youtube.com/watch?v=InXyEE27XlU
   Interactive Scenario with Powerpoint (medium video)
      https://www.youtube.com/watch?v=IOoVim0HBaU
   Branching Scenario tutorial (short overview video)
      https://www.youtube.com/watch?v=wIJUIikSJxY

Creating interactive scenarios (branched scenarios) with Google forms:
   https://www.youtube.com/watch?v=culjr3SB7rA
   https://www.youtube.com/watch?v=_vz1jiB7qRI&t=1s

Resource to assist you in getting started (A helpful blog with several hyperlinks for more info):
   http://blogs.articulate.com/rapid-elearning/building-scenarios-for-e-learning/

References

Kuhlmann, T. (2009, July 14). Building Branched E-Learning Scenarios in Three Simple Steps. Retrieved from https://blogs.articulate.com/rapid-elearning/build-branched-e-learning-scenarios-in-three-simple-steps/

Mary A. Sciaraffa, Eastern Kentucky University

Using Students' Second Language to Tackle Prejudice and Misconceptions

In my experience as a professor of both linguistics and Spanish grammar courses, I find language prejudices to be particularly impervious to questioning. Though they typically serve as proxies for biases that connect directly to race, ethnicity, socioeconomic status, and gender (see, e.g., Campbell-Kibler, 2012), individual speakers (in this case, students) rarely recognize them as such. For most students, prescriptive norms and standard speech are often seen as inherently correct and grammatically logical, while non-standard speech is taken to reveal intellectual deficiencies or a willful ignorance of "the rules" on the part of the non-standard speaker (Pullum, 1999).

Interestingly, this tendency to see grammar as inflexible stems in part from how it is taught in educational settings (Larsen-Freeman, 2001). Many educators conceive of grammar rules as immutable characteristics of language, and students often learn that only certain forms of communication are acceptable in speech and writing. While standard forms of speech do have a place in professional and educational settings, the complete rejection of the notion that non-standard forms are linguistically valid ignores decades of insights by experts in the field of language research.

For this reason, "[t]he linguistic[s] classroom presents a unique opportunity for raising student awareness about diversity and multiculturalism" (Gooden, 2007, p. 102) and for dismantling prejudice. This situation is especially true when the lessons of the linguistics classroom focus on students' second language, for which they often have limited or non-existent prejudices. Students' general lack of sociolinguistic bias about their second language allows them to appreciate the complexity and diversity of natural variation in another language without judging the speakers who employ certain variants. Characteristics like grammatical complexity, diversity across communities, and natural variation within communities are in fact inherent to all varieties of human language (Labov, 1972), but they are often obscured by socially-based – rather than linguistically-based – ideas regarding "appropriate" or "correct" forms of speech.

When students eventually do learn of the social prejudices associated with the complex grammatical patterns they learn about, they are often perplexed by the inconsistency of the judgments regarding linguistic innovation, conservatism, complexity, change, and variation in their second language. Having not yet been immersed in the social environments that give rise to such biases, students have the rare opportunity to approach the study of distinctive linguistic traits with a relative *tabula rasa*, socio-linguistically speaking. The process of learning about variation in their second language can also help them to recognize and reassess the validity of any native-language biases they might have. This awareness creates an opportunity to open up discussions about parallels in English and other languages and leads students to critically analyze their beliefs about language.

References

Campbell-Kibler, K. (2012). The implicit association test and sociolinguistic meaning. *Lingua, 122*(7), 753–763. http://doi.org/https://doi.org/10.1016/j.lingua.2012.01.002

Gooden, S. (2007). Diversity in the linguistic classroom. In J. Branche, J. W. Mullennix, & E. R. Cohn (Eds.), *Diversity across the curriculum: A guide for faculty in higher education* (pp. 102–106). Bolton, MA: Anker Publishing Company.

Labov, W. (1972). *Sociolinguistic patterns*. Philadelphia, PA: University of Pennsylvania Press.

Larsen-Freeman, D. (2001). The grammar of choice. In E. Hinkel & S. Fotos (Eds.), *New Perspectives on Grammar Teaching in Second Language Classrooms* (pp. 105–120). New York: Routledge.

Pullum, G. (1999). African-American vernacular English is not standard english with mistakes. *The Workings of Language*. Retrieved from http://www.lel.ed.ac.uk/~gpullum/aave-not-mistakes.pdf

Colleen Balukas, Ball State University

VII. Service-Learning/ Community-Based Learning

The following are characteristics of this HIP:

- The classroom is moved from the institution to the community.
- Students both apply what they are learning to a real-world setting and reflect upon it.
- Giving something back to the community provides the student with a good model for future citizenship.

This section contains six articles. Is service learning possible and/or appropriate for your discipline? What about the classes you actually teach?

Making Play Not Just for Fun:
A Service-Learning Project in a Children's Museum

Play and the Children's Museum

The importance of play to children and how play contributes to their cognitive, social/emotional, language, and motor development have been addressed through the years (Howard & McInnes, 2013). A children's museum is a place where children are allowed to freely experience play and explore. The Interactive Neighborhood for Kids, Inc. (INK) is a non-profit organization located in Gainesville, Georgia. The mission of INK is to develop the full potential of children from ages 2 to 12 by providing a rich environment, where children are allowed to freely explore their dreams and unlimited ideas. Different exhibit rooms in the museum (e.g., Medical Clinic, Radiology Department, Dentist Office, SunTrust Bank, Beauty Salon, Goods Grocery Store, Post Office, Courtroom, 50s Café, Vet Clinic, etc.) are designed for children to explore and experience various career possibilities. Moreover, INK has developed a partnership with the University of North Georgia for several years.

Course Information

EDUC 2130 (Exploring Learning and Teaching) is one of the required education foundation courses in the core curriculum. This course enables students to explore the key aspects of educational psychology, including learning theories, developmentally appropriate pedagogical strategies, student learning motivations, factors that impact students' learning, student diversity, and effective educational environments. The goal of this course is to allow future educators to apply their knowledge of teaching and learning to enhance the learning of students who have various backgrounds in a variety of contexts. A 20-hour field experience is necessary to fulfill the requirement of this course.

Purpose and Procedures of the Service-Learning Project

A successful service-learning project aids students to connect to the world around them (McDonald & Dominguez, 2015). The purpose of this service-learning project is to allow pre-service teachers to apply the knowledge of teaching and learning discussed in class into the field, thereby facilitating children's play, optimizing children's learning, and making play considerably meaningful.

The students were instructed to design age-appropriate learning activities that teach children about different career opportunities. The following procedure is used to conduct the service-learning project.

1. Select a focused exhibit room and determine the corresponding career cluster.
2. Formulate ideas and plans for a hands-on activity (10–15 minutes) for children in the focused exhibit room. The activity should introduce the work of professionals, such as post officers, nurses, dentists, vets, police officers, restaurant managers, and musicians, among others.
3. Consolidate ideas into a lesson plan that includes the objectives and step-by-step procedures for the activity.
4. Use the knowledge of teaching and learning learned from the course to justify the selected activities and instructional strategies.
5. Implement plans in the field. Complete the 20-hour field experience.
6. Complete a final reflection paper.

Examples of Designed Activities

50s Café Restaurant

K guided the children to decide and play different roles, including cooks and waiters/waitresses. K instructed them to develop their own menus for the guests. The children drew different pictures of food that they wanted to serve on construction paper. K pretended to be a guest and ordered food from the menu prepared by the children. Accordingly, the children used their imagination to make different plates and serve their guests.

Radiology Room

T brought numerous insect X-ray and picture cards to the radiology room. Several boys were interested in the cards and wanted to explore the X-ray light board. T explained what an X-ray is and its function. T placed several insect X-ray cards on top of the X-ray light board. The boys attempted to determine which insect pictures matched the X-ray cards. Given the near physical similarities of a few insects, the children discussed among themselves the characteristics of the different insects.

Food Grocery Store

H prepared a set of paper money to engage children in a shopping game. She introduced the work of checkout clerks and store staff members. The children took turns to put the groceries in the child-sized shopping cart, check out at the register, and place items back to their proper places based on the category of the food. While children were scanning the grocery items, H integrated mathematics concepts into the activity by asking "What is 3 dollars plus 4 equal to?" or "How much change should you give me?"

Impact of the Project on the Students

This project provides opportunities for students to apply content knowledge into the field, interact with different children, understand the critical roles of adult support in children's learning, and contribute to their community.

> "I noticed that not all students learn the same way, and some students need different instructions in order for them to self-motivate themselves."
> - Casey

> "When you do something it is not just benefiting you but it is making an impact on the person around you…INK really showed me how important it was to make the little things matter."
> - Jushua

> "Almost everything that I was taught in class and everything that I read in my textbook was relevant at INK. It is refreshing to actually be able to witness what you learned and read in class to what you experience in real life."
> - Colby

References

Howard, J., & McInnes, K. (2013). *The essence of play: A practice companion for professionals working with children and young people.* New York, NY: Routledge.

McDonald, J., & Dominguez, L. A. (2015). Developing university and community partnerships: A critical piece of successful service learning. *Journal of College Science Teaching, 44(3)*, 51-56.

Yen-Chun Lin, University of North Georgia

University-Level Factors Affecting Outcomes of Community-Based Learning

Recognizing its positive impact on student learning, colleges are increasingly implementing community-based learning (CBL). CBL provides students with opportunities to apply the material they learn in a real-world setting. CBL opportunities range from job shadowing, to community service, to field trips. Due to this wide range, CBL provides varying levels of student involvement, ranging from simple observation to solving problems that impact their communities. CBL experiences not only help shape how students critically think while they are in school, but provide positive learning effects years after graduation (Moely & Ilustre, 2016).

Students who participate in CBL programs are more likely to develop better inter- and intrapersonal skills, increase their overall grade point average, improve their higher-level critical thinking, and obtain a more nuanced perspective of the world (Engin, 2014). CBL thus provides meaningful learning on both a personal and professional level (Hart & Akhurst, 2017).

While community-based programs can provide rich opportunities for students, certain aspects of CBL have been shown to be ineffective or even detrimental. One such instance can occur when students, often unwittingly, view such learning experiences through the lens of cultural voyeurism. Rather than viewing a community problem as something to be fixed collaboratively, they see it as something they can step in and fix themselves. Naturally, this disempowering outsider interference approach has problematic consequences for all involved (Hart & Akhurst, 2017). Alternatively, students can "rubber-neck" and observe real-life problems without any intent to meaningfully understand or solve the problem. A related problem can occur when students take too narrow of an approach to CBL. This limited perspective happens most often when students are required to find a solution to a community problem for part of their course grade. Through a combination of tight time constraints and unrealistic goals, students often fall short of what they intended to accomplish (LeCompte & Blevins, 2015). Likewise, students may expect a CBL to end as the semester does, but community members may feel betrayed and used by students' abrupt departure.

To create the best possible outcomes to CBL, researchers recommend having a series of ongoing conversations that occur both in and out of the classroom with students and with the populations they hope to help. These conversations have been shown to enlighten students of their own perspectives and biases as well as assist them in realizing the strengths and values of the broader community (Engin, 2014). Another remedy to the potential problem of exploitation is to have a frank talk with students before they embark on these projects. Openly discuss time constraints to ensure that realistic plans and goals are set. Additionally, to minimize the risks of exploitation, clearly explain what students are, and are not, expected to do. Providing students with such guidelines in writing is most beneficial.

The most significant contributing factor to the success of CBL is faculty involvement. Faculty chose to participate in CBL experiences because they can find ongoing professional development opportunities, can publicize their service-learning accomplishments, and can learn new technical innovations (Russell-Stamp, 2015). Professors are more likely to view CBL as a valuable use of their time when they are aware of community resources and perceive support from their colleagues, administrators, and the community as a whole. The use of campus CBL offices can assist with preparing meaningful CBL experiences, establish ways of assessing student work, build community connections for placement, and address concerns about the learning environment (Russell-Stamp, 2015). Because of these benefits, faculty members typically enjoy working with a campus CBL office.

When done effectively, CBL experiences can have lasting effects on students, extending long past their college career. Students learn to become more engaged and experienced advocates, and the community gains more people with direct knowledge of its problems and potential ways to solve them (LeCompte & Blevins, 2015). Thus, meaningful, well-planned CBL experiences serve to integrate the university with its broader community, a win for all individuals involved in the process.

References

Engin, M. (2014). Preparing students for community-based learning using an asset based approach. *Journal of The Scholarship of Teaching & Learning, 14*(5), 48-61. doi:10.14434/josotlv14i5.5060

Hart, A., & Akhurst, J. (2017). Community-based learning and critical community psychology practice: Conducive and corrosive aspects. *Journal of Community & Applied Social Psychology, 27*(1), 3-15.

LeCompte, K., & Blevins, B. (2015). Building civic bridges: Community-centered action civics. *Social Studies, 106*(5), 209-217.

Moely, B. E., & Ilustre, V. (2016). Outcomes for students completing a university public service graduation requirement: Phase 3 of a longitudinal study. *Michigan Journal of Community Service Learning, 22*(2), 16-30.

Russell-Stamp, M. (2015). Faculty use of community-based learning: What factors really matter? *Michigan Journal of Community Service Learning, 21*(2), 37-48.

Stepteau-Watson, D. (2012). Infusing student activism into the college curriculum: A report of a service-learning project to bring awareness to sexual violence. *College Student Journal, 46*(4), 788-794.

Sara Halcomb, Spalding University
Lauren Holder, Spalding University

Changing Lives and Minds: A Win-Win

When teaching health psychology, I [Nathaniel] realize it is difficult for students to understand the complexity of health care systems in which patients find themselves. Additionally, unless they have personal experience with serious illness/disability, many students have little insight into the experience of patients. To this end, I developed a service-learning requirement for my advanced health psychology course to enhance knowledge of health care systems and patient experience.

Students must complete 12 hours of volunteer service at a medical-related facility during a 16 week semester. Students frequently choose pediatric hospitals, skilled nursing facilities, rehabilitation facilities, hospitals, emergency rooms, free clinics, specialized clinics (e.g., HIV clinic)—anywhere patients find themselves regularly interacting with medical professionals. Although students often choose to volunteer at the type of facility where they believe they would like to work, I often encourage the "unsure" student to volunteer where I believe need is greatest, skilled nursing facilities (often referred to as nursing homes).

I have found that approximately half of my students initially balk at the idea of adding one more requirement to their already complex and busy lives. While this is understandable, I discuss the importance of the assignment, provide anonymous written reactions from previous students, and make sure the assignment is weighted with the proper amount of points to reflect the time commitment.

Here are the assignment requirements:
1. Students must keep a log of when they volunteered, signed by an organizational representative at the end of the 12 hours.
2. Students must keep a detailed journal. I require them to split up the 12 hours into at least four sessions to make the volunteering more meaningful. Students are asked to journal after each of their four volunteer sessions. I have "bent a little" on this requirement if the student makes a compelling argument why

their learning will not suffer by completing the hours in fewer than four sessions. I ask them to journal their thoughts and feelings during each volunteer session. I typically ask them to write at least one page per journal entry.
3. Students must NOT engage in 'therapy' or psychological interventions, but rather just be a "thoughtful volunteer."
4. Students must write a final reflection regarding their entire experience. I provide some of the following prompts:
    a. What is the environment like for medical staff?
    b. What is the environment like for patients?
    c. How did medical staff interact with one another? What are your reactions to these interactions?
    d. How did medical staff interact with patients? What are your reactions to these interactions?
    e. What is the most powerful "patient story/experience" you encountered and how will it influence your future work?
    f. How could a health psychologist in that facility improve the lives of staff and patients?
    g. How did you as a volunteer improve the lives of staff and patients?

Many students report the service learning experience to be one of their most influential/meaningful assignments in their education. Anecdotally, about a third continue to volunteer after the semester ends. Some students observe what they perceive as injustices in patient care and are motivated to change the system. Some students marvel at the level of care and respect provided to patients. Every student has a unique experience navigating these complex systems, just as each patient has a unique experience navigating these complex systems. Most importantly, students walk away from the assignment knowing far more about health care systems, patient experiences, and how just a little thoughtful time and energy on their part can make a difference in someone's life.

Nathanael Mitchell, Spalding University
Robin K. Morgan, Indiana University Southeast

Tiered Journaling: Multiple Paths to Reflecting on Service Learning

Background

Reflection has long been established as a key ingredient to a transformative service learning experience (Eyler, 2002; Sedlak, Doheny, Panthofer, & Anaya, 2003). It helps undergraduates contextualize their education and enables them to gain perspective on academic learning outcomes. To tap into reflection, instructors frequently assign writing in a journal, with students keeping an account of activities and their impact on intellectual, emotional, and social growth. Bringle and Hatcher (1999) apply theories from Dewey and Kolb to create a list of "types of reflective journals," including *key phrase journals* (integrate identified terms into entries), *double-entry journals* (describe experiences on the left, discuss how the experiences connect to course content on the right), and *critical incident journals* (articulate an incident or situation that created a dilemma, analyze choices, and suggest a course of action). In my planning of a new community-based experience for pre-service teachers, journaling was designed to leverage the advantages from a variety of these techniques.

The Experience: Creating a Documentary

As part of a field experience focusing on the public's knowledge of Science, Technology, Engineering, and Mathematics (STEM), juniors in a mathematics education course were required to create a documentary with original source interviews and filmed activities. The project was designed: (1) to determine adults' level of understanding concerning K-12 state standards for STEM content, (2) to create and present informational activities (math lessons) showcasing the state standards, (3) to assess the impact of these sessions on participants' perceptions of content and pedagogy. In addition to planning lessons, the preservice students developed the protocols for individual and focus group interviews and independently produced a twenty-two-minute video that mixed recordings from diverse settings and populations (a makerspace foundry, a local library, and a community center with a high percentage of displaced adults and families). Throughout the twelve-week endeavor, the students engaged in reflection via a tiered journaling process.

Reflecting on the Experience: Tiered Journaling

Tiered journaling afforded students an opportunity to convey their thoughts, feelings, and beliefs in a variety of ways, including both written and audio entries. Students used MicroSoft OneNote as a repository for their reflections, with access to all work provided to the instructor. For audio-recordings that involved more than one pre-service student, files were set to open access for all appropriate parties. The following table provides a brief overview of the four types of assignments that comprised the tiered journal:

Assignment	Mode	Frequency
Pre-Experience Goals	Written (Structured, Polished)	Weekly
Rationale/Instructions (1) Outline what you hope to accomplish on the project for the week **and** (2) Describe any questions or concerns that you have as you enter into this week's work. This should be proof-read and polished writing.		
Impromptu Reactions	Written or Audio Recording (Unstructured, Raw)	As Desired
This is "free-thinking" space. If you need to decompress or unleash some energy, grab a pen and paper, a tablet or computer, or your smartphone. Note: if necessary, scan jottings into OneNote. Impromptu reactions may be particularly helpful *while working on and/or after* accomplishing the week's goals. These should be raw, unedited entries.		
Self-Guided Focus Groups	Audio Recording (Semi-structured, Raw)	Four Checkpoints
In groups of three or four, record a conversation that addresses how the service learning experience is contributing to the goals of the course. You can also discuss any issues related to the service learning experience (for example: "I like …" "I wish …" "I wonder …").		
Analysis and Synthesis	Written (Structured, Polished)	Mid-Semester, End of Semester
Analyze the benefits and drawbacks to the service-learning experience. Include when and where have you found the most fulfillment in terms of professional growth (with explication) **and** how the experience has/not influenced your future-teaching-self. This should be proof-read and polished writing.		

Reflections and Implications

After only one year of implementation, anecdotal evidence indicates that undergraduates find tiered journaling to be beneficial: both as an analytic tool for introspection and as a way to connect theory, practice, and audience. The juniors, on end-of-semester course evaluations, commented that "knowing exactly when to let your imagination and thoughts flow and when to use a critical approach made it easier to go beyond just recounting activities."

"Honesty here. I used voice recordings for all my journaling. But, and this is huge, I had the computer transcribe to text and that forced me to proof-read and reflect on entries. In the past, I'd just type and either try to get it right the first time or not worry about what came out."

"To beat a dead metaphor, this way of journaling was really eye-opening in that I could really see (and hear) how my ideas were changing over time.'"

"It was good to be able to have a variety of ways to journal. What surprised me is how the self-guided focus often led to debates about the nature of math. We weren't just talking about how people learn or what to do to convince people about its importance. These became talks about mathematics itself."

"After our library workshop, two people from the audience heard us [students] planning for our focus recording and wanted to know if they could join us! I thought that was really neat, but didn't know what to say."

These excerpts, along with pre-student-teaching screening interviews, suggest that this service learning experience has helped to contextualize the importance of conveying content standards to a wide audience. The undergraduates recognize that personal understanding of principles for teaching and learning mathematics is only a small piece to the puzzle of changing community norms. In fact, being agile with delivery of the subject and understanding differences in public perception will continue to be critical to this new generation of teachers. And although this exercise was conducted in a teacher education program, it is worth noting that the ideas and procedures can work for any service learning course looking to promote reflection in (and on) the field.

References

Dewey, J. (1933). *How we think: A restatement of the relation of reflective thinking to the educative process.* Boston, MA: Heath and Company.

Kolb, D. A. (1984). *Experiential learning: Experience as the source of learning and development.* Englewood Cliffs, NJ: Prentice-Hall.

Bringle, R. G., & Hatcher, J.A. (1999). Reflection in service learning: Making meaning of experience. *Educational Horizons, 77*(4), 179-185.

Eyler, J. (2002). Reflection: Linking service and learning - Linking students and communities. *Journal of Social Issues, 58*(3), 517--534.

Sedlak, C. A., Doheny, M. O., Panthofer, N., & Anaya, E. (2003). Critical thinking in students' service-learning experiences. *College Teaching, 51*(3), 99-103.

Jeffrey P. Smith, Otterbein University

Service-Learning in the Visual Arts

Service-Learning is one of the eleven High-Impact Practices identified by Kuh (2008). Kuh described service-learning as field-based cooperation with the community as part of a particular course to future the objectives of a course and assist the community through a project designed for them. Teaching through service-learning provides an effective hands-on approach for authentic learning experiences for higher education students. The service-learning experience benefits multiple stakeholders. The students, community guests, and the university bookstore were able to cooperate to benefit elementary school students as a special day was created for them. This task required flexibility, fluidity, risk-taking and organizing 'behind the scenes' for all stakeholders. It has been found to be a successful method that fosters research through the visual arts to prepare preservice students as they develop their teacher skills. Regarding excellence in visual arts teaching, the National Arts Education Association (2016), states that "In the process, the teachers not only enabled students to develop their artists skills and understand the art world; they also helped students learn from their mistakes and envision new solutions" (p. 1).

Entering a university course in arts education methods can be nerve-racking for some preservice students preparing to teach through visual art, especially if students are more familiar with finding 'only one right answer'. Some students may not have embarked in original art-making since a 5th grade art class. Some students entering may not see themselves as 'creative' problem-solvers or successful collaborators. However, teaching through service-learning at the university gallery helps students better understand teaching methods, how to make connections through gallery collections, and hot to apply art methods and collaborative skills in our visual age.

Our service-learning project involves students enrolled in an art methods course in a teacher preparation program at the University. The university students develop original art samples to be used during a community day at the university bookstore. These samples are carefully designed with links to standards and interdisciplinary content through studio methods. The community day is linked to The Dr. Seuss events, which align with "Read Across America" to integrate literary skills and art. Students work in teams to build an art lesson plan with aims and outcomes linked to standards of learning.

Before the day of the event, at the university gallery, students write higher level thinking questions aimed to engage young learners. Planning is an essential part of teacher preparation, and field work of visiting the university gallery prepares the university student for inquiry using collections. The goal of the interaction with the elementary age students is to help them to look at visual art and find personal connections while engaging in higher level thinking through conversations in the gallery. The university students build divergent questions and develop a gallery 'guide' for inquiry using the levels of Bloom's Taxonomy.

On the day of the event our festive engaging learning endeavor begins with costumed guests appearing as the "Cat in the Hat" with face painters and red and white Seuss-style hats for all. The costumed guests read to small groups of elementary age students. Each team of university students then begins an art lesson with the children. The teaching experience provides the opportunity for students to work with young learners in an art activity that is hands on and student centered as well as conducting gallery tours for children and families. Through service-learning, our gallery becomes an effective learning environment in which learner centered, knowledge centered, arts based, and community centered elements interact. The event lasts for 4 hours. During that time period the university students lead the elementary students through story reading, art projects, and gallery tours.

Student outcomes include collaborative experiences, a model for creating projects, the fostering of originality and problem-solving abilities, finding value in diverse solutions, building positive relationships in the community, and developing a teaching style. Sharing and reflection are keys to understanding first-hand what works/what does not and why? How do I modify a plan? What did children create, and what does that mean for that child?

After teaching, the students post images and their reflections, a practice that is directly applicable to the profession as teachers. University students revise their plans. Students build a personal 'tool kit' to pull from what is uniquely their own. The event fosters opportunities to create, research, write, revise, reflect, refine, and share. Students take away a personal final digital portfolio of images to use in job interviews, to share as research at the undergraduate symposium, and/or to share at state conferences.

In our teaching for mastery, service-learning allows for growth and revision in an authentic way, a building of 21st century skills sets in collaboration, creativity, community, and critical thinking with enduring outcomes. The students are on a path that values high quality teaching and risk-taking through visual art as rising, more confident future educators.

References

Kuh, G. D. (2008). Excerpt from high-impact educational practices: What they are, who has access to them, and why they matter. Association of American Colleges and Universities.

National Art Education Association. (2016). *Learning in a visual age: The critical importance of visual arts education.* National Art Education Association.

Patti Edwards, Old Dominion University
Joyce Armstrong, Old Dominion University

Highlight Your Students' Work: Art Show (but not by artists)!

I teach our introductory computer programming course utilizing a multimedia computation approach, where we teach computer science concepts by having the students write programs to manipulate images and sounds. This approach provides a context for learning computer science concepts. Soon after I started teaching the course, I read a short article about another university holding a public viewing of the "art" collages the students in their programming course had created. I liked the prospect of highlighting the work our beginning students were doing and wanted to make it more public. I was able to gain support from the department chair and other course instructors.

Thus started our all-section "Art Show," where the best student-created photo collages (a project midway through the course) are selected from each section and publicly exhibited each semester. The process I established mimics the submission of a manuscript to a peer-reviewed journal, where peers select the best for publication, and the authors have an opportunity to make minor improvements in their work based on the peer review. This show raises visibility of the department within the University and provides a venue in which students can highlight their work to their peers and others. It also highlights the ability to be creative in a computer science degree program. Many of the students are motivated to be creative and more engaged beyond simply completing the requirements for the project.

To start with, this is a middle-of-the-semester project the students submit for a grade. Students write a program that creates a picture collage of modified images. The project is open-ended in that they can create any image they want, but the completed program and collage must meet a set of minimum requirements to earn full credit. In addition to the project being assessed, every collage created by the submitted projects is judged by the students within that section of the course. (We typically have three to five sections each semester.) Those collages selected as the best from each section advance to a public all-section art show. Further judging occurs at this level by department professors and individuals from other parts of the university, with awards being given for the best collages.

For nine semesters so far, I have organized and promoted this event, which has become a department tradition. Each semester I create a supporting show handout, an entrant web page, and a web page documenting the winners (the website can be viewed at http://www.cs.bsu.edu/homepages/dllargent/CS120ArtShow.html). Each semester, I also create and post printed panels that contain the all-section art show winners for that semester. I post the two most recent semesters' panels in a highly-visible display case in a first-floor hallway of one of our instructional buildings. Older panels are framed and hanging in a computer science classroom in the same building. The display of these panels provides local public recognition for the students' work indefinitely and locally promotes what the department has to offer. Students often state the art show was a highlight of the course and kept them engaged.

The all-section art show has occasionally garnered local print media attention. I have recently entered into a partnership with our university library to establish a digital media repository that will provide open and free access to submitted student work from the art show project. This repository will provide public recognition for the students' work, and promote what the department has to offer to a significantly wider audience. All students in the course are encouraged to submit their art show work for archiving.

Details and Logistics

A variety of activities go into making this whole process a success, including the following items.

Section judging: We have two rounds of in-class peer (student) voting. I print out each collage in color on a half sheet of paper and tape them to the wall around the room on voting day. All submissions are entered in round one. Roughly the top third advance to the second round of student voting, which determines the entries that advance to the all-section art show. We have 15-25% of the students from each section advance. The percentage varies because of the limited space we have in our public venue; we strive to have roughly 25 entrants. The selected students are given four days to make minor improvements to their program based on grading feedback and resubmit it for the all-section art show. Each entrant is required to sign a FERPA release form.

Poster creation: A poster for each entrant is created by graduate assistants or instructors. Each poster includes the student's name, a title for their collage, an 8.5" x 11" color print of the collage, a small print of the original image(s) used, and the program that creates the collage.

Attendance: I do not hold class on the day of the show, but rather require the students to attend the show long enough to sign an attendance sheet. Most students stay much longer and enjoy looking at other sections' submissions. This gathering also allows the students whose submissions are being displayed to be present and thus interact with those looking at their collages.

Judging: I recruit a variety of judges: computer science professors, professors from other departments, administrators, and sometimes upper-division students. All judges are asked to evaluate each entry on an aesthetics level. Judges with a programming background are also asked to evaluate the code quality. After the show, I send a thank you card to each judge.

Show handout/web page: The show handout contains a thumbnail of the collage image, the student's name, major, and a brief artist statement for each entry. I also create a webpage showing all entries to the show with the same information as is provided in the handout. After the show, I create a webpage to honor the winners.

Promotion: I reach out to our school and our community newspapers to provide details about the all-section art show. Occasionally, we have been covered, so I keep notifying them. We also send out an e-mail notice to the entire campus.

David L. Largent, Ball State University

VIII. Internships

The following are characteristics of this HIP:
- Internships provide students with glimpses of their future by immersing them in an actual work setting.
- Internships allow students to be coached by professionals in the field in addition to professors in the classroom.
- The best internships have an academic component wherein students write and reflect upon their work experience.

This section contains three articles. Are internships not only appropriate but available in your discipline? From a critical thinking perspective, do you see any disadvantages to internships in your discipline?

Why an Internship

Internship provides students and budding professionals an opportunity to experience the work of their chosen field first-hand and practice their skills and knowledge in a functional and meaningful way. Internship experiences are unique in their ability to combine classroom learning with on-the-job training, and become even more beneficial when paired with frequent and high-quality supervision. This essay will outline the key benefits to internships as well as delineate the key factors that make some internship experiences more successful than others.

Benefits to Internship

Career Benefits: Having a variety of internship or experiential learning experiences can provide students and prospective employees an advantage in the skills they have to offer to potential employers (Beard & Morton, 1999). Internships provide learning experiences that cannot be directly substituted for by coursework and grades, and therefore individuals who enter the workforce with a variety of on-site training and practice often outshine applicant counterparts. In some instances, internships can even lead to a job opportunity at the company in which one interns.

Career Focus: In addition to providing students with an opportunity to practice useful career-specific skills, internships can also provide opportunities for students to clarify their career goals (Beard & Morton, 1999; O'Neill, 2010). For example, students who are uncertain of their career goals may gain insight into if they should pursue a different career goal or continue with their current ambitions.

Compensation: Many internship sites offer limited compensation opportunities for student interns, which can result in a variety of mixed reactions. Some students may feel they are working for "free" or being asked to put forth considerable time and effort for little payback. Professors can help by reminding students that most internships offer benefits beyond financial compensation. Internships can often be worth college credit, and thus reduce the amount of time required of them in the classroom (Beard & Morton, 1999). Additionally, some sites may offer employee discounts or even provide a financial stipend for student time.

Networking: In addition to providing students an opportunity to build skills and knowledge, internships and other immersion work experiences can introduce students to the types of contacts and services in their field, as well as provide them with introductions to field innovators (Beard & Morton, 1999). These contacts can be useful in future career development, as well as offering possible references and future colleagues.

Qualities of a Successful Internship

Training. The best internships not only provide unique training opportunities to enhance students' skills, but also support the student growth (O'Neill, 2010). Offering a planful, sequenced, developmentally appropriate training program is a hallmark of the best internships. Whether the training is one-on-one or in a group is unimportant; the key is that the overall quality of training is top priority.

Meaningful Work. Internships are best when they provide opportunities to do meaningful work to expand students' knowledge and resume (O'Neill, 2010). What is meaningful for each student may differ; however, having a positive internship experience increases student engagement, learning, and satisfaction. Internships that focus on having students do "grunt" work (e.g., data entry; clerical work) are not perceived as valuable from students' perspectives and serve to decrease student motivation.

Clear Expectations: The most beneficial internship opportunities are those in which the parameters and expectations of the internship are clear and well understood, both by the student intern and by the internship site (O'Neill, 2010). Providing expectations and guidelines ensures that learning and experience goals of the student are met while also making it more likely that the student meets the needs and goals of the internship.

Good Supervision: Internships provide opportunities to practice and fine-tune skills that will be later used throughout one's career. The key to ensuring that these practiced skills are the best possible is frequent and high-quality supervision by an expert in the field (Beard & Morton, 1999). Having one or more supervisors at an internship site is crucial to learning, practice, and growth. One of the most important qualities of good supervision is for the student to receive regular feedback (O'Neill, 2010). Numerous avenues of feedback ensure that the student can ask questions as well as correct any performance issues. Additional qualities of a good supervisor include: specific direction and feedback, positive encouragement instead of criticism, respectful communication, support of intern autonomy and growth, open communication, and feedback between the supervisor and educational institution (O'Neill, 2010).

Multiple Opportunities: Research has shown that students who complete multiple internship or experiential learning opportunities report feeling better prepared and more competent in their skills (Coker & Porter, 2015; O'Neill, 2010). The students' career development identity increases with each subsequent internship experience by improving students' confidence in their skills as well as providing them with a multitude of experiences and viewpoints. These varied experiences lead to a broader, more well-rounded learning experience.

Diversity: Internships should ideally provide the students opportunities to engage with people who are different from themselves (O'Neill, 2010). Ideally, students would then reflect on their own experiences to become more culturally competent. Regardless of a student's career path or chosen field, becoming competent with a diverse range of cultures is crucial in our ever-changing society.

Access: Due to the significant benefits offered to students who undergo internships, all students need equal access to these experiences (Coker & Porter, 2015). Some students may have compounding factors outside of their school life, such as family demands, jobs, disabilities, or other factors that could affect their ability to take some internships. Providing the opportunity for a variety of options enables more students to take advantage of internship opportunities regardless of compounding situational demands.

Internships provide invaluable opportunities for students in their personal and occupational growth. However, not all internships are created equal, with some proving to be more beneficial than others. Ensuring quality support, training, and experiences for students offers the best outcome for both students and internship sites.

References

Beard, F., & Morton, L. (1999). *Effects of internship predictors on successful field experience. Journalism & Mass Communication Educator*, 53(4), 42-53.

Coker, J. S., & Porter, D. J. (2015). Maximizing experiential learning for student success. *Change*, 47(1), 66-72.

O'Neill, N. (2010). Internships as a high-impact practice: Some reflections on quality. *Peer Review*, 12 (4). Retrieved from: https://www.aacu.org/publicationsresearch/periodicals/internships-high-impact-practice-some-reflections-quality

Katelyn Federico, Spalding University
Sabrina Kordes, Spalding University

One Size Doesn't Fit All

We encourage students to complete either an internship, a research project, or both prior to graduating. Many of our students choose an internship as they perceive this option as allowing them to develop more practical, work-related skills. Students can work with our Career Services office to locate an internship or can find an internship site on their own. All internship sites will have an on-site supervisor. In addition, a faculty supervisor is provided for each intern. Faculty serving as internship supervisors vary tremendously in how they interact with their interns. Typically, faculty are told to ask interns to keep a daily journal for what they do at their internship site, complete assigned readings, meet with them every two weeks, and write a reflection of their experience. Over the years, I [Robin] have discovered that a slight variation of these requirements might best serve students.

As a psychology professor, I find that many of my internship students are placed in positions where they have interactions with clients. Most frequently, these interactions involve caretaking duties and, occasionally, providing entry-level therapeutic services, including implementing behavioral treatment plans. Invariably, students discover what they learn in their classrooms isn't always what they see implemented onsite. My challenge became providing students supervision that addressed their specific needs within the context of the expectations of the program. Two modifications led to enhanced student satisfaction with supervision and a greater sense of connectedness between what they were learning at the University and what they were experiencing on-site. These two modifications led to a more tailored approach with little to no additional work for the instructor.

- Modification One: The use of a daily journal for students to record their experiences at the internship site is a common one. Over the years, I expanded this requirement, asking students to record their behaviors onsite (what they did and what they observed), their thoughts (what they thought about what they did and observed), and their feelings (how did they feel about what they did and observed). By my expanding the daily journal to include thoughts and feelings, the daily journal became an ongoing reflection about their internship site providing greater detail about their experience and eliminating the need for an additional reflection assignment at the end of the internship. At our university, students are already asked to provide an end-of-the-semester reflection at their internship site and for Career Services; completing a third reflection for the faculty supervisor was an added burden to the student and an added grading chore for the faculty member.
- Modification Two: In the past, students completing an internship under my supervision were asked to read a standard collection of articles. These articles had been accumulated across professors and were general discussions about internships, their advantages to students, and general information learned from completing internships. Although useful, these articles did not appear to assist students in connecting what they were learning in the classroom with what they were experiencing onsite. Instead, when meeting with students, I began

reviewing their entries, discussing with them areas of comfort and areas where they lacked knowledge. For example, one student worked in a setting with many children diagnosed on the autism spectrum. Her onsite supervisor was using sensory integration therapy. As a result of her questions about this treatment approach, I provided her articles describing a wide range of treatments for those diagnosed on the autism spectrum. She read the articles, wrote summaries in her journal, and then we discussed the information in future meetings. This just-in-time approach to providing information helped her make sense of what she was seeing onsite, and our discussions helped her understand not only what research has shown about effective and ineffective treatments for those diagnosed on the autism spectrum but also the challenges of working in a setting where treatments may not match the research evidence.

Providing supervision for students completing internships must assist students in navigating both academic and their own anxieties. By revising the daily journal assignment to include greater reflection and then tailoring assigned readings to the needs of the individual student, supervision can play a significant role in helping students be successful. (686 words)

Robin K. Morgan, Indiana University Southeast
Nathanael Mitchell, Spalding University

Internships with Impact: Secondary Mathematics Teacher Education

Kuh and O'Donnell (2013) defined the following high impact practices for internships:
1. Performance expectations set at appropriately high levels
2. Significant investment of time and effort by students over an extended period of time
3. Interactions with faculty and peers about substantive matters

4. Experiences with diversity wherein students are exposed to and must contend with people and circumstances that differ from those with which students are familiar
5. Frequent, timely, and constructive feedback.
6. Periodic, structured opportunities to reflect and integrate learning
7. Opportunities to discover relevance of learning through real-world applications
8. Public demonstration of competence (p. 10)

This teaching tip describes strategies for implementing high-impact practices within a secondary mathematics methods course and an accompanying internship in a teacher education program. Senior-level undergraduates complete a series of activities within a mathematics methods course for preservice secondary mathematics teachers that culminates with demonstration of teaching competence through public performance and the production of a portfolio, including video. Students must demonstrate knowledge and skills as this is the single methods course that they will experience before student teaching. The sequence of activities shown and described below seeks to build the skills needed to successfully plan, teach, and assess in the secondary classroom:

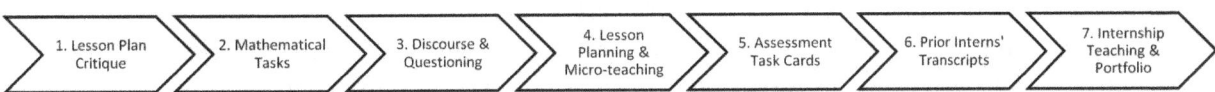

Figure 1: High Impact Practices within an Internship in a Secondary Mathematics Methods Course.

Lesson Plan Critique—Students begin by selecting what they consider at the course outset to be an effective lesson plan for teaching high school mathematics. Students are provided with a 2-page format for critiquing the lesson plan. Two example lesson plans are provided to students that have been critiqued using this technique. The critique is dispersed throughout the lesson plan, using red text. The critique requires students to look at the lesson description, learning goals and objectives, required resources and materials, instructional procedures, guiding questions, and assessment and evaluation. Students also read *Making Sense of Mathematics for Teaching* (Nolan, Dixon, Safi, & Haciomeroglu, 2016), highlighting the *TQE Process: Tasks, Questioning, and Evidence* (pp. 7-9). The task goal is for students to understand that their first judgment of what constitutes a quality lesson plan may not be a sound one grounded in scholarship about effective teaching.

Mathematical Tasks & Problem Solving—Students engage in discussion concerning the differences between true mathematical problems for students, discussions that require novel thought processes versus problems that are exercises requiring them to replicate processes. Students are introduced to the *Mathematical Task Framework* (Stein & Smith, 1998). Using technological tools and algebra tiles (Nolan, Dixon, Safi, & Haciomeroglu, 2016, p. 46), they probe particular mathematical ideas deeply, such as quadratic functions, examining sources that require them to consider multiple representations of the concept, using technological tools and algebra tiles (Nolan, Dixon, Safi, & Haciomeroglu, 2016, p. 46). The key is that the students need to experience mathematics that they believe they already know in a novel and new context.

Discourse and Questioning—Students participate in a series of Paideia seminars concerning classroom discourse and questioning involving mathematics. "A Paideia Seminar is a collaborative, intellectual dialogue facilitated with open-ended questions about a text" (National Paideia Center, para. 1). The seminars' purpose is to provide preservice teachers with models of effective mathematical discourse and questioning as portrayed in articles describing lessons from real classrooms. These articles show examples of sound discourse and questioning practices as well as examples of less effective practices that one may see enacted. Specific question stems and strategies for creating effective mathematical discussions are discussed (Cirillio, 2013; Herbel-Eisenmann & Breyfogle, 2005; Manouchehri & Lapp, 2003; Springer & Dick, 2006; Stein, 2007). As students engage in the Paideia seminars, the instructor withdraws, and the seminar participants engage in a deep text discussion.

Lesson planning and micro-teaching—Students work in pairs to produce a series of lesson plans using a provided format (Allen, 2017). Segments of these lessons are presented to their peers, a strategy called micro-teaching. At the conclusion of micro-teaching, students are asked to provide feedback to one another. The instructor conducts an after-lesson debrief with the class to discuss issues ranging from speaking too softly, to issues pertaining to the accuracy of the mathematical content or the appropriateness of the instructional activity to the lesson's goals and objectives. Students are provided with opportunities to practice skills they will need as a teacher. The public performance aspect is crucial.

Assessment task cards—Students examine problems from the *NAEP Questions Tool* from the National Assessment of Educational Progress. They examine model task cards that demonstrate how to: create problems; design rubrics for assessing student work; and create brief commentaries that document probable student misconceptions. Students must produce task cards that are displayed and discussed in class. This task assists them in developing the skills necessary to create materials that will allow them to evaluate the effectiveness of their instruction.

Analysis of transcripts of student lessons—Prior to students entering high schools for internships, they analyze a series of transcripts taken by the university supervisor concerning lessons taught by interns during prior semesters. By analyzing these lesson transcripts, prospective teachers learn: 1) common mistakes that novice teachers of mathematics make, and how to avoid them; and 2) what lesson expectations are and what type of written and oral feedback they can expect from their cooperating teacher and university supervisor.

Internship teaching and portfolio—Students engage in an internship where they teach a series of lessons in a high school and produce a teaching portfolio that includes the lessons, instructional activities, student assessments including students' work and their feedback to the students, and the intern's reflections concerning their teaching. High impact practices within the internship provide students with opportunities to: 1) recognize the relevance of information learned within college classrooms, and; 2) demonstrate their competence in applying that knowledge within the profession. Employing high impact practices embedded in the internship allows teacher candidates to learn to exhibit skills and behaviors that will be necessary for success as they proceed into student teaching the following semester.

References

Cirillo, M. (2013). Discussion research brief: What are some strategies for facilitating productive classroom discussions? Reston, VA: National Council of Teachers of Mathematics. http://www.nctm.org/Research-and-Advocacy/Research-Brief-and-Clips/Strategies-for-Discussion/

Herbel-Eisenmann, B. & Breyfogle, M.L. (2005). Questioning our patterns of questioning. *Mathematics Teaching in the Middle School, 10*(9), 484-489.

Kuh, G.D. & K. O'Donnell (2013). *Ensuring quality & taking high-impact practices to scale.* Washington, DC: Association of American Colleges and Universities.

Manouchehri, A. &Lapp, D. (2003). Unveiling student understanding: The role of questioning in instruction. *Mathematics Teacher 96*(8), 562-566.

NAEP Questions Tool. National Assessment of Education Progress. Washington, DC: National Center for Education Statistics. https://nces.ed.gov/nationsreportcard/nqt/

Paideia National Center (2017). What is Paideia Seminar? In *Paideia: Active Learning.* Retrieved from https://www.paideia.org/paideia-seminar/

Springer, G.T. & Dick, T. (2006). Making the right (discourse) moves: Facilitating discussions in the mathematics classroom. *Mathematics Teacher, 100*(2), 105-109.

Stein, C. (2007). Let's talk: Promoting mathematical discourse in the classroom. *Mathematics Teacher, 101*(4), 285-289.

Stein, M.K. & Smith, M.S. (1998). Mathematical tasks as a framework for reflection: From research to practice. *Mathematics Teaching in the Middle School, 3*(4), 268-275.

Tracy Goodson-Espy, Appalachian State University
Diana Moss, Appalachian State University
Ashley Whitehead, Appalachian State University

IX. Capstone Courses and Projects

The following are characteristics of this HIP:
- These courses/projects function as final exams for the discipline.
- These courses/projects integrate and apply what students believe they have learned.
- The final project takes many forms—research, a portfolio, a performance, an exhibit—depending upon the discipline.

This section contains six articles. Since each discipline chooses its own type of project, is there anything new you have learned about such projects that might be applied to your discipline? How comprehensive should the project be relative to the entire discipline's curriculum?

Motivating Students to Learn with Project-Based Learning

Think back to your own college and graduate education and what assignments contributed most to your learning. These memorable assignments were likely dissertations, capstone projects, laboratory experiments, and semester-long multi-tiered group projects. These projects exemplify Project-Based Learning (PBL). Project-based learning encourages students to critically apply the knowledge they learned in classes in a real-world practice. PBL has been found to increase many critical, meta-cognitive skills, including problem solving, time management, collaboration, flexibility, organization, metacognition, and responsibility (Wurdinger & Qureshi, 2015).

In order for students to receive the most benefits of PBL, teachers must implement certain evidence-based teaching techniques. A successful PBL project creates a situation that encourages students to use a trial-and-error approach to assess their successes and failures by receiving feedback from the teacher using scaffolded instruction (Barak & Dori, 2009; Hmelo-Silver, Duncan, & Chinn, 2007). When students are effectively guided and supported in this way, it can reduce their cognitive load, so that they are less overwhelmed, thus maximizing their learning potential (Hmelo-Silver, et al., 2007; Bell, 2010). Adding an element of autonomy in PBL is also critical so that students can develop a sense of ownership and control over their learning (Helle, Tynjälä, & Olkinuora, E., 2006).

So, let's break it down further. How does a professor promote autonomy while still providing direction and support in the PBL experience? By finding the perfect blend of these two critical factors throughout each of the three phases of PBL. The first phase involves the ***project launch***, which enables students to gain an understanding of the overarching goal or driving question, and identify what knowledge is needed to achieve desired results. The students then autonomously choose the specific topic to investigate, after which the teacher provides feedback and offers a list of timing milestones to help students stay on track. The students view these milestones as larger goals, and create smaller stepping stones to reach them (English & Kitsantas, 2013). This process is consistent with the PBL goal of self-regulated learning, while providing substantial support and feedback.

Phase two of the PBL model involves using ***guided inquiry and solution creation***. This phase often consumes the majority of the student's time and work. In this stage, students gather information, assign meaning, and reflect on or monitor their progress. The teacher assumes the role of a guide, as opposed to an instructor, to foster the students' independent learning. In addition to guiding students' learning, the teacher also encourages student-initiated dialogue to promote critical thinking and ownership of the learning process. This strategy allows the teacher to provide specific individualized feedback without wrestling control from the student (English & Kitsantas, 2013).

Phase three is unique to PBL. The first two phases in this model are consistent with *problem*-based learning, which allows students to synthesize their knowledge by solving an open-ended problem. However, *project*-based learning involves an additional phase. This final phase allows the students to **present their findings and reflect** on the results and the learning process. Keeping with the model of teacher as guide, the teacher should facilitate a discussion during which students focus on what they learned, how they did or did not achieve their goals, and how their results and processes compared to those of their peers (English & Kitsantas, 2013).

As the students are assessing their progress throughout the process, the teacher should also assess their progress in tandem. The criterion upon which students are judged should be presented prior to the project's onset, so that students can self-reflect on their development and experience. The grading criterion should clearly explain what is expected of students as they work in groups and evaluate them based on their active participation and collaboration. When presented in this manner, PBL has been found to improve academic goal setting and performance (English & Kitsantas, 2013; Hao, Branch, & Jensen, 2016).

When all three stages are properly implemented, PBL has been found to be effective in all phases of schooling from elementary to higher education (Kokotsaki, Menzies, & Wiggins, 2016). An individual understanding of one's students is critical to utilizing PBL, as some students may require more hands-on involvement from a teacher than more autonomous others (English & Kitsantas, 2013). Requiring students to think critically and apply their knowledge to real-world problems has been shown to improve academic performance, attendance, and cooperative learning skills (Edutopia, 2001). As such, PBL is recognized as one of the most effective techniques to fostering student learning (Hao, Branch, & Jensen, 2016), and thus can be an enriching activity for both teacher and student.

References

Barak, M., & Dori, Y. J. (2009). Enhancing higher order thinking skills among in-service science teachers via embedded assessment. *Journal of Science Teacher Education, 20*(5), 459-474.

Bell, S. (2010). Project-based learning for the 21st century: Skills for the future. *The Clearing House, 83*(2), 39-43.

Edutopia. The George Lucas Education Foundation. (2001). Project-based learning research. Retrieved October 20, 2016, from http:// www.edutopia.org/php/article.php?id=Art_887&key=037)

English, M. C., & Kitsantas, A. (2013). Supporting student self-regulated learning in problem-and project-based learning. *Interdisciplinary Journal of Problem-Based Learning, 7(2),* 6.

Hao, Q., Branch, R. M., & Jensen, L. (2016). The effect of pre-commitment on student achievement within a technology-rich, project-based learning environment. *TechTrends, 60(5),* 442-448.

Helle, L., Tynjälä, P., & Olkinuora, E. (2006). Project-based learning in post-secondary education–theory, practice and rubber sling shots. *Higher Education, 51(2),* 287-314.

Hmelo-Silver, C. E., Duncan, R. G., & Chinn, C. A. (2007). Scaffolding and achievement in problem-based and inquiry learning: A response to Kirschner, Sweller, and Clark (2006). *Educational Psychologist, 42(2),* 99-107.

Kokotsaki, D., Menzies, V., & Wiggins, A. (2016). Project-based learning: A review of the literature. *Improving Schools, 19(3),* 267-277.

Wurdinger, S., & Qureshi, M. (2015). Enhancing college students' life skills through project-based learning. *Innovative Higher Education, 40(3),* 279-286.

Autumn Truss, Spalding University
Anna Grace Cooper, Spalding University

The Power of Reflection: The "Thought-Piece" in Capstone Courses

Guess what, capstone courses are important. Culminating capstone experiences help students engage in professional development opportunities, reflect on their time in college, and create environments to summarize and bring closure to the college experience. Capstone courses, typically taken near the end of students' college programs, are offered both departmentally and, increasingly, through general education. Ultimately, capstone courses are designed to bridge the gap as students transition from the undergraduate role to post-graduation roles (Rowles, Koch, Hundley, & Hamilton, 2004).

One important element of high-impact practices is the chance for students to have periodic and structured opportunities to reflect and integrate learning (Kuh & O'Donnell, 2013). As a high-impact practice, according to the AAC&U, capstone classes are wonderful instructional platforms that allow students to write, create, research, build portfolios, discuss, and **reflect**. Reflections help students make holistic sense of their education by applying and summarizing what they have learned throughout their program.

Our activity reinforces two aspects of the capstone. First, portfolio building. Second, **reflection**. As part of their coursework in our capstone classes, students can compile a portfolio that requires writing multiple essays on the collegiate experience. Specifically, students complete the following assignments: (a) Personal Statement/Biographical Sketch; (b) Career Thought Piece; (c) Cover Letter; (d) Resume; (e) Learning from Work Experience Thought Piece; (f) Learning From Coursework Thought Piece; (g) Learning From Activities Thought Piece; (h) Ethics Thought Piece; (i) Diversity Thought Piece; (j) Overview of Department Experience; and (j) Reflection on the Capstone Project.

We want to spend the remainder of this entry explaining each reflection and mini-assignment that could be employed as part of a capstone experience.

1. The **Personal Statement/Biographical Sketch and Career Thought Piece** are used by professors during one-on-one student meetings early in the semester. These meetings enhance the professor-student relationship.
2. The **Resume and Cover Letter** are used as part of a mock interview assignment that requires students to meet with a campus representative in Career Services.
3. The **Learning from Work Experience, Coursework, and Activities Thought Pieces** require students to reflect on two or more related experiences and how they created learning opportunities that students may incorporate into answers during job interviews.
4. The **Diversity Thought Piece** allows students to ponder the multicultural nature of society while reflecting on personal biases or blind spots.
5. The **Ethics Thought Piece** allows students to define their personal ethics while reflecting on how their collegiate experience influenced and, perhaps, altered these views.
6. The **Overview of Department Experience** allows students to discuss positives and negatives related to their university experience with a specific focus within their major.

The thought pieces are explained in more detail below.

Learning from Work Experience Thought Piece

Experience and *learning* are not the same thing. It is possible to have an experience and learn nothing from it. This thought piece provides students an opportunity to reflect upon key experiences and what was gained from them. Students must select relevant work experiences (full-time, part-time, internships, etc.), and describe what they learned in each position. Students should write about two-three different jobs.

Learning from Coursework Thought Piece

Students should select a transformative training experience (e.g. courses, workshops) that resulted in learning directly applicable to their performance as a college student. The reflection should be, at minimum, one-page. Students should provide at least one-two examples.

Learning from Activities Thought Piece

Students consider transformative activities outside of conventional work/training (e.g., hobbies, travel, and community/social service) that they have accumulated. They should, specifically, select one example and write a one-page reflection.

Diversity Thought Piece

Students will write a one-page essay about their views regarding valuing and managing diversity. Students should be thoughtful and critical in their responses. Some questions to consider include, but are not limited to:
- What has been your experience with the "global community?"
- What are your ethnocentricities?
- Have your views changed throughout your college career?
- How have your views on this issue transformed?

Ethics Reflection

Students will write a one-two page essay outlining their ethical values as a communicator. Be thoughtful and critical in your response. Some questions to consider include, but are not limited to:
- What, to you, constitutes ethical communication?
- What standards do you and will you live by in your interactions with others?
- Have your views changed throughout your college career?
- How have your views on this issue transformed?

Overview of Department Experience Reflection

Students can write a one-two page essay about their collegiate experience with most of the emphasis being on their "major" department.

The capstone is first and foremost a high-impact practice, but it is also a culminating student experience. Therefore, it is important that students reflect on their time as a student, specifically how they applied critical thinking, what they learned, and how they were transformed.

References

Kuh, G.D, & O'Donnell, K. (2013). *Ensuring quality and taking high-impact practices to scale*. Washington, DC: Association of American Colleges and Universities.

Rowles, C., Koch, D., Hundley, S., & Hamilton, S. (2004). Toward a model for capstone experience: Mountaintops, magnets, and mandates. *Assessment Update, 16*, 1-2.

Michael G. Strawser, Bellarmine University
Jason M. Martin, University of Missouri Kansas City

Preparing Preservice Teachers for edTPA: Frustrations and Tips for Teacher Educators

As part of our elementary education senior mathematics methods course, *Teaching Mathematics in Elementary School,* preservice teachers are required to develop two lesson plans and implement them during their field experience. This requirement allows preservice teachers to enact the content and pedagogy they have learned about during their three-course mathematics methods sequence, while under supervision of their cooperating teacher in their field placement. These two mathematics lessons help prepare preservice teachers for their culminating assessment – the Teacher Performance Assessment (known as edTPA) – which is a national assessment used to determine if beginning teachers are ready to teach. (Stanford Center for Assessment, Learning, & Equity; SCALE, 2016).

In order to prepare preservice teachers for the student teaching edTPA requirement, our elementary education program has developed edTPA Lite, the purpose of which is to scaffold for the official edTPA. During their senior elementary mathematics methods course, preservice teachers conduct a practice edTPA, which will be scored using the edTPA rubrics. This culminating assignment was created in order to provide support to preservice teachers, as outlined on the edTPA website's FAQ (Pearson Education, 2017). For example, as teacher educators we can provide access to: handbooks, scoring rubrics, examples (with permission), and help students with their writing and performance in certain areas. However, we may not help preservice teachers during the student teaching edTPA submission process by offering critiques, providing feedback, or even helping choose their video clips to use for submission. Therefore, by providing support in a "Lite" format the semester prior to student teaching, we are able to support our students as they prepare for their culminating assessment.

While implementation of the official edTPA is still in its early stages at our university, so is our edTPA Lite assignment. In addition to the two lessons preservice teachers create, they are asked to complete the three task commentaries: focusing on planning, instruction, and assessment, as practice for when they complete their actual edTPA during their final semester. Together these three tasks "represent a cycle of effective teaching" (p.2), and provide evidence of the lesson and student learning through the provided artifacts and written commentary (see figure 1).

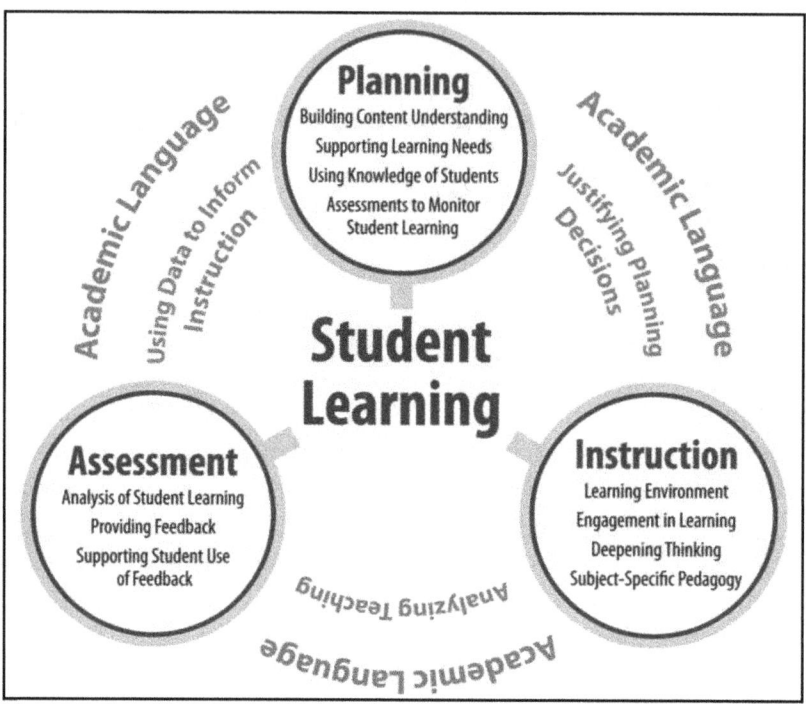

Figure 1. (SCALE, p. 2)

Since this assignment was piloted during the Fall of 2017, we are delineating frustrations we have encountered, as well as tips for others who might want to implement such an assignment with their own preservice teachers. These frustrations and tips are not exhaustive of all one might encounter, and are limited to our students and their experiences with the assignment. However, they do serve as a stepping stone for a discussion on how to improve the assignment for future semesters.

Frustrations:

1. Time and Support. While writing the practice commentaries requires more time and effort from the preservice teachers, it also requires more time and support from teacher educators. For example, additional time spent grading the lengthy commentaries is added onto the regular class assignments for the course. Additionally, by providing the support, we lose class time to the discussion of edTPA formalities (i.e. task templates, language, requirements) that would otherwise be used for more content and pedagogy.
2. Stress. During their senior year, students are often stressed by the amount of work each class demands of them. On top of this work, they are now teaching and video-taping lessons for the first time. Many worry about teaching for the first time and feel they may cause misconceptions or negatively affect their students' understanding.
3. Focus on writing. While the purpose of edTPA is to have preservice teachers demonstrate they are capable of planning and implementing a mathematics lesson, as well as assessing student learning, oftentimes this goal can get lost when they are trying to use appropriate language functions, demands, and syntax when writing their commentaries. This loss of focus causes frustration for teacher educators as we try to provide support in their writing, as well as frustration for preservice teachers as they work to write enough to provide evidence for the grading rubrics.

Tips for Successfully Implementing edTPA Lite:

1. Plan together. Allow preservice teachers to plan their lessons together, if possible. Since this is one of the first times they will be teaching, this collaboration allows them to support one another's' ideas and to think through tasks that are high-level (Smith & Stein, 1998; Stein & Smith, 1998) and researched-based for their students. Pragmatically, it allows more time for the instructor, as she will not have to grade multiple lessons on the same topic.
2. Create realistic expectations. In order to alleviate stress and pressure, we have created a similar scoring rubric, using the ones from edTPA, but set the expectation that students are learning and will not achieve perfect products the first time. For example, students are required to achieve a 4 or 5 in order to get an A+, a 3 for an A-, 2 for a B, and 1 for a C. This action helps take the pressure off of students and allows them to focus on doing their job – learning how to teach students.
3. Provide multiple avenues of support. One way in which teacher educators can support preservice teachers during the edTPA Lite process is to remind them of the ideas they have learned about in class (i.e., high-level tasks, modifying

lessons for diverse learners) and help them make connections to what is being asked of them to write about in their commentaries. Furthermore, asking students to provide support as peer reviewers for one another, attend workshops on edTPA writing, or referring them to writing centers can provide additional support.

Again, while these frustrations and tips are not comprehensive, it is our hope that teacher educators can have support to help prepare their preservice teachers for edTPA. While edTPA is important to our students in order to gain licensure, edTPA Lite should not take over the purpose of the course. Instead, the lesson plans and reflections should be natural components of the course that are highlighted in order to help students in their edTPA process.

References

Pearson Education (2017). *Frequently Asked Questions.* Retrieved from http://www.edtpa.com/PageView.aspx?f=GEN_FAQ.html

Smith, M. S., & Stein, M. K. (1998). Selecting and creating mathematical tasks: From research to practice. *Mathematics Teaching In The Middle School, 3*(5), 344-50.

Stanford Center for Assessment, Learning, and Equity (SCALE), (2016). *Elementary mathematics assessment handbook.* Board of Trustees of the Leland Stanford Junior University.

Stein, M. K., & Smith, M. S. (1998). Mathematical tasks as a framework for reflection: From research to practice. *Mathematics Teaching In The Middle School,* (4), 268-275.

Ashley Whitehead, Appalachian State University
Chrystal Dean, Appalachian State University
Lisa Poling, Appalachian State University

Effective Utilization of a Capstone Project: A Case Study Oral Exam

A capstone project can play an integral role in synthesizing material learned throughout a student's degree program. For professional graduate programs such as counseling or other health professions an oral exam case study can be an ideal real world high-impact practice that asks students to demonstrate clinical skills and decision making. The following tip will describe how faculty in a rehabilitation counseling program use an oral exam case study to assess individual student learning and program outcomes.

Oral Exam Case Study Format

Students are eligible to complete the oral exam in their last semester of the program. Throughout the program students are provided opportunities to prepare for and practice the oral exam case study. Most courses use case studies as a means to introduce and reinforce curriculum standards. In addition, students are also required to do oral presentations and mini oral exams to practice articulating their knowledge. Being able to analyze a case file and articulate an action plan are essential skills rehabilitation counselors will use in their everyday practice.

The day of the oral exam, students are presented with a case study, instructions, and a rubric. The average case study is approximately 500-600 words. Students have one hour to prepare and can use any materials (computer, notes, & books) to help build their rehabilitation plan. Students present their plan to three faculty, and each case study uses the same scenario. The student is a new partner in a rehabilitation counseling agency, and they are presenting their rehabilitation plan (based on the case study) to the other partners in a staffing.

Students have approximately 20 minutes to present their rehabilitation plan. When the students are finished presenting, the faculty ask the students questions based on their plan. Typical questions ask students to defend their treatment rationale, are any ethical considerations, how does culture impact the rehabilitation goals, can you role play a counseling theory, and/or what community agencies could be a referral. Once all questions have been answered, the student steps out of the room, and the faculty grade the oral exam using a rubric with four domains (theoretical perspective, professional orientation & ethics, case formulation, and career development). Students are brought back into the room, told their result, and are provided with feedback. Students can pass, fail, pass conditionally, and pass with distinction. During the feedback process, students are asked to reflect on their performance and develop professional goals to instill lifelong learning. The average oral exam takes approximately one hour and forty-five minutes to complete (1-hour preparation time and 45 minutes to present and answer questions).

Assessment

The rubric has a 1(low) to 5 (high) scale, and students who score 10 or below fail, 11-12 pass conditionally, 13-16 pass, and 17 or above pass with distinction. Student who fail are given extensive feedback, another case study to reinforce the feedback, and then schedule another oral exam to demonstrate new learning. Generally, students who pass conditionally have one area to improve. These students are provided feedback and then meet with a faculty member to discuss how they incorporated the feedback into their learning.

Data are recorded on each of the domains and as a total score. Three of the domains (theoretical perspective, professional orientation & ethics, and career development) are core program competencies. The data are reviewed annually as part of the program's assessment plan. The data is shared with multiple stakeholders, including the program's dean, Vice President for Academic Affairs, advisory committee, and accreditation body. Based on the results, changes to courses and assignments may be considered.

The faculty value the oral exam format as a unique means to "see" student thinking in real time. It provides additional evidence of student learning, enhancing more common assessments like papers, projects, and exams. Most importantly, the oral exam case study allows students to fully integrate their learning using authentic procedures they will use in their everyday practice.

Michael Kiener, Maryville University of St. Louis

Using Graduate Level Action Research to Impact Teacher Effectiveness and Student Achievement

TELL data suggest that some Kentucky schools are not effectively using action research as a beneficial model for professional learning. After entering the workforce, newly graduated teachers find limited opportunities to engage in critically reflective activities about their educational practice. Action research is an attractive option for teacher researchers, school administrative staff, and other stakeholders in the teaching and learning environment to consider (Mills, 2011). Action research encourages collaboration, teacher reflection, and change in schools. Calhoun (1994) describes action research as a fancy way of saying "Let's study what's happening in our school and decide how to make it a better place." The University of the Cumberlands Teacher Leader and Literacy

Specialist programs believe that action research is an essential component in improving both teacher effectiveness and student learning.

In their final course of the programs, all Teacher Leader and Literacy Specialist candidates are required to address a problem of practice at either the classroom level, PLC, or school level. Candidates serving in P-12 school settings are asked to identify a problem of practice, develop and implement an action research plan, and collect and analyze data. Finally, the action research project, along with the reflection/analysis, is presented by the candidate to the local school community, district, or public forum of choice.

Over five-hundred candidates, in the Teacher Leader and Literacy Specialist programs have embarked on the action research journey. It has been very rewarding to see the impact our candidates are making on student achievement. Survey data indicates that graduates see the effect these programs are having on their abilities to impact professional learning and student achievement through the action research process.

References

Calhoun, E.F. (1994). *How to use action research in the self-renewing school.* Alexandria, VA: Association for Supervision and Curriculum Instruction.

Mills, G.E. (2011). *Action research: A guide for the teacher researcher* (4th ed.). Boston: Pearson.

Jennifer Chambers, University of the Cumberlands

From Paper to Social Networking: Updating Capstone Assignments for the Electronic Age

Capstone courses serve three functions within academia. First, they facilitate students' personal reflection, allowing them the chance to consider which of the skills and concepts learned in school may be leveraged in future academic and/or professional endeavors. Second, they provide students with the opportunity to consider how the concepts mastered within their prescribed curriculum may be extended and showcased in the professional world. Finally, they provide students with an occasion to consider and develop their own professional identity, which may be introduced to prospective colleagues via professional socialization activities (van Acker & Baily, 2011).

The creation of a comprehensive resume is common within many capstone courses (McGann & Cahill, 2005). This assignment provides students with the opportunity to reflect upon and highlight their academic achievements, specific field knowledge, and non-academic endeavors, which position them well to be successful in the professional realm. While the exercise of creating a resume may be an important step in transitioning from undergraduate studies to the professional world, some argue it reflects outdated application practices, given society's increasing attention to and use of technology, including social networking sites (Nikolaou, 2014; Roth, Boko, Van Iddekinge, & thatcher, 2013).

One way to update this assignment may be to more explicitly integrate technology into it, such as via the development of a comprehensive LinkedIn profile. LinkedIn is perhaps best described as a 'social platform for professionals'. It allows people to highlight their knowledge, skills, and experience while simultaneously facilitating opportunities to connect with other professionals. The platform allows its users to seek and provide endorsements from others, which strengthens their perceived professional status. LinkedIn also allows its members the opportunity to share media, participate in professional online groups, engage in forum discussions, review job postings, and to send private messages, making it a dynamic tool for connecting with other professionals. The platform is often utilized by recruiters, as well, to locate potential hires (Bohnert & Ross, 2010; LinkedIn, 2017). In 2017, LinkedIn had over 467 billion users worldwide with over 3 million job postings at any given time (Chaudhary, 2017). Encouraging students to create a well-developed LinkedIn profile may directly propel them into the job market, allowing students to connect with professionals at a much faster pace than more traditional strategies (e.g., the creation of a paper resume).

The development of an effective LinkedIn profile requires intention as well as professional savvy. The first step in creating a notable profile is to optimize the headline. This step is especially important, as this headline is included within the Google Index and will appear in both searches and others' newsfeeds. Given that students will, in most cases, be emerging professionals, the headline does not need to be limited to a job title. Instead, one may consider using this area of the profile to highlight personal qualities he or she maintains, problems he or she solves, etc. Next, the summary section of one's profile allows individuals the opportunity to introduce themselves to viewers by providing a narrative regarding their experiences, goals, desires, or whatever else they would like to highlight for the reader. Students should craft this portion of their profiles to serve as a summary, of sorts, covering the information they might typically emphasize in their cover letters.

Beyond the summary, there are three main areas included in a basic LinkedIn profile: 1) background, 2) skills, and 3) accomplishments. Within the 'Background' section of one's profile, work experience, education and volunteer experience may be showcased. All experiences should be included in this area, including those which might best be classified as 'temporary' or 'contractual'. Students should use the 'Skills' section of the profile to identify their abilities secondary to formal training or experiences. This formal identification of proficiencies allows students to be discovered in specific skill-related searches conducted by recruiters and those in similar positions. Further, skill designations allow students' connections the opportunity to endorse them for those skills, which, in turn, should increase their perceived professional standings. Within the final section of the profile, the 'Accomplishments' section, students may list publications, presentations, certifications, courses, projects, honors and awards, patents, test scores, language proficiencies, and affiliations with various organizations. This section may be particularly important to those with little real-world experience, as it allows students to highlight their efforts to increase knowledge and skills, which will prepare them to excel in real-world endeavors offered to them (LinkedIn, 2017). Instructors may want to break the development of one's profile into four separate assignments, each focused on one major area of the profile.

Once completed, students need to ensure the accuracy of their profiles. Dates included on the profile should be accurate, as should position descriptions, noted achievements, and skills utilized. Equally important is the manner in which the information is presented. Students should be advised regarding the importance of using proper spelling and grammar. Remind students that this is their first introduction to potential employers, mentors, and collaborators. As such, one's first impression, as conveyed via the LinkedIn profile, matters. To aid in the viewer's positive perception of the profile, students should include a headshot that portrays them in professional attire. This picture should take up approximately 60% of the frame allotted (Baert, 2017). Given that most students will have limited experience to highlight, it may make sense for them to access the 'Edit' mode within the profile to rearrange the profile sections. For example, perhaps the student wants to present academic achievements prior to work experience. Or, perhaps he or she would like to provide a comprehensive summary before providing the viewer regarding specific details regarding his or her strengths, experiences, and abilities. Students should also consider deleting non-applicable sections that seem to weaken their profiles. While making modifications to their profiles, students should consider accessing the *Privacy* options menu within their account to mark 'No' under 'Share Profile Edits'. This option allows individuals to make modifications to their profiles without alerting others to the editing process (Bohnert & Ross, 2010; LinkedIn, 2017).

Developing a well-developed profile is only one step in effectively using the LinkedIn platform. Once the profile is ready to share, individuals are then tasked with growing their networks. Students may grow their networks by searching for those with whom they have studied or worked, for those whom engage in the industry they wish to pursue, or with those with whom they hope to collaborate. As students identify appropriate connections, they may add those individuals to their network. Personalizing requests to connect (rather than relying on auto generated messages) typically facilitates greater response rates. It may also serve as the first opportunity to introduce one's self authentically to the recipient. Just as one requests to join others' networks, they should consider accepting all reasonable requests as well. The larger one's LinkedIn network is, the more searchable he or she becomes. As a matter of proper etiquette, students should also thank people for adding them to their networks, as they notice the same occurring. This option not only conveys a minimum level of professionalism, but also helps the individual to stand out from others who may not make such an effort.

Building one's network is an excellent start to establishing a professional presence. It is incumbent upon the LinkedIn user, however, to actively engage with the platform. Students should be advised that approximately 40% of LinkedIn users search their newsfeeds on a daily basis (Chaudhary, 2017). As such, it is important for students to generate new content so that others may increase awareness of them. Only minor (but regular) actions are required to stay active in one's newsfeed. Individuals may share, like, or comment on posts in their feed to generate activity. Sharing original content is important, as well. A final strategy for building one's LinkedIn profile is to seek the endorsements and recommendations of others. Having one's skills endorsed by others increases the individual's perceived expertise in a particular area. Similarly, specific recommendations allows one's audience to see how others value his or her skillset. Perhaps the most effective (and expedient) way to secure others' endorsements and recommendation is to provide them to others. Students should take the time to offer thoughtful, authentic, and comprehensive recommendations to others. Further, they should also be advised that there is an option to 'Request a Recommendation' from others as well.

Instructors may further leverage this assignment by grouping students to peer-review each other's profiles. This strategy not only allows them insight into how other students highlight similar experiences and knowledge, but also will allow them the opportunity to begin building their own professional networks via the platform.

References

Baert, S. (2017). Facebook profile picture appearance affects recruiters' first hiring decisions. *News, Media, and Society*. https://doi.org/10.1177/1461444816687294

Bohnert, D., & Ross, W.H. (2010), "The influence of social networking web sites on the evaluation of job candidates," *Cyberpsychology, Behavior, and Social Networking, 13*(3), 341-347. doi: 10.1089/cyber.2009.0193.

Chaudhary, M. (2017). LinkedIn by the numbers: 2017 statistics. Retrieved from https://www.linkedin.com/pulse/linkedin-numbers-2017-statistics-meenakshi-chaudhary/

LinkedIn. (2017). How LinkedIn can help you. Retrieved from: https://www.linkedin.com/help/linkedin/answer/45/how-linkedin-can-help-you?lang=en

McGann, S., & Cahill, M.A. (2005). Pulling it all together as is capstone course for the 21st Century emphasizing experiential and conceptual aspects, soft skills, and career readiness, *Issues in Information Systems, 6*(1), 391-397.

Nikolaou, I. (2014), Social networking web sites in job search and employee recruitment. *Int J Select Assess, 22*, 179–189. 10.1111/ijsa.12067

Roth, P.L., Bobko, P., Van Iddekinge, C.H. & Thatcher, J.B. (2013). Social media in employee-selection-related decisions: A research agenda for uncharted territory," *Journal of Management, 42*(1), 269-298. doi: 10.1177/0149206313503018.

van Acker, L., & Baily, J. (2011). Embedding graduate skills in capstone courses, *Asian Social Science, 7*(4), 69-74.

Sara Bender, Central Washington University

X. ePortfolios

The following are characteristics of this HIP:
- This practice makes student learning more visible and connected.
- The practice employs the combination of guided reflection and networked digital technology.
- This practice allows for measurement of students' progress throughout their academic careers.

This section contains three articles. Does your discipline currently employ ePortfolios? If not, is it possible to adapt the ePortfolio to your curriculum?

Six-Word Stories – A Simple, Powerful Portfolio Reflection Tool

Introduction

The legend of the six-word story goes back to a challenge issued to Ernest Hemingway to author a story in six words. Hemingway met the challenge with the story "For sale: baby shoes, never worn."[1] Today, you can find examples of six-word stories throughout the Internet. A project of note in the six-word community is Michele Norris' "The Race Card Project"[2] Norris uses six-word stories to explore and dialogue issues around race challenges in this country.

Portfolios and their use within education settings predate the "Hemingway legend"; think about artists maintaining their portfolios during the Renaissance. In 2016 "e-portfolios" (the digital offspring of "portfolios") were determined to be a "high impact practice" (HIP).[3] As a HIP, e-portfolios have gained increasing traction as a critical tool in supporting teaching and learning practices within the higher education community

Portfolios at University of Alaska Anchorage

In 2014, the University of Alaska Anchorage (UAA) formerly launched a university-wide e-portfolio initiative. In December of that year, UAA executed a multi-year contract with Digication to provide e-portfolio services.[4] As the portfolio project matured within the University, discussions began with Native Student Services (NSS) to incorporate portfolio-based services in their programming. This effort led to the development of the Native Cultural Identity ePortfolio work that has received national attention.[5]

Introducing Six-Word Stories at UAA

By invitation in the fall of 2015 from the Native Student Services staff members, Tommy Lee Woon, formerly a multicultural education dean at Stanford and Dartmouth Universities, began a collaboration with NSS to explore and develop approaches around e-portfolios, Native identity development, and overcoming historical trauma; Mr. Woon shared his initial reflections on this work in a 2016 "eFlection" - https://youtu.be/hotbtyIPFM0 .

On his first visit to UAA, Woon introduced NSS staff, Sheila Randazzo and Cheryl Turner to the idea and use of six-word stories as a powerful way to give "voice" to Native students. His first workshop with Native students focused on the prompt, "Develop a six-word story that captures a time that you felt like you belonged." The response to the exercise was overwhelmingly positive with animated sharing by students!

Our team introduced e-portfolios after this event and every subsequent six-word story event to show students how to digitally memorialize their stories. This action helped Native participants of all ages learn how to extend through technology the valued Native tradition of storytelling for sharing wisdom, healing, and remembering ancestors.

Connecting Six-Word Stories, Reflections, and e-Portfolios

Often individual e-portfolios and their associated reflections are envisioned as large-scale "museums of self" with dozens of artifacts showcased across multiple pages and sections. An example from UAA is Osama Abaza's robust e-portfolio available here - http://bit.ly/2yJz8xD. In the context of our six-word story work, however, an e-portfolio is a much simpler undertaking and includes only: the six-word story, an image, and a short reflection (some story details) – that's it! Here's an example:

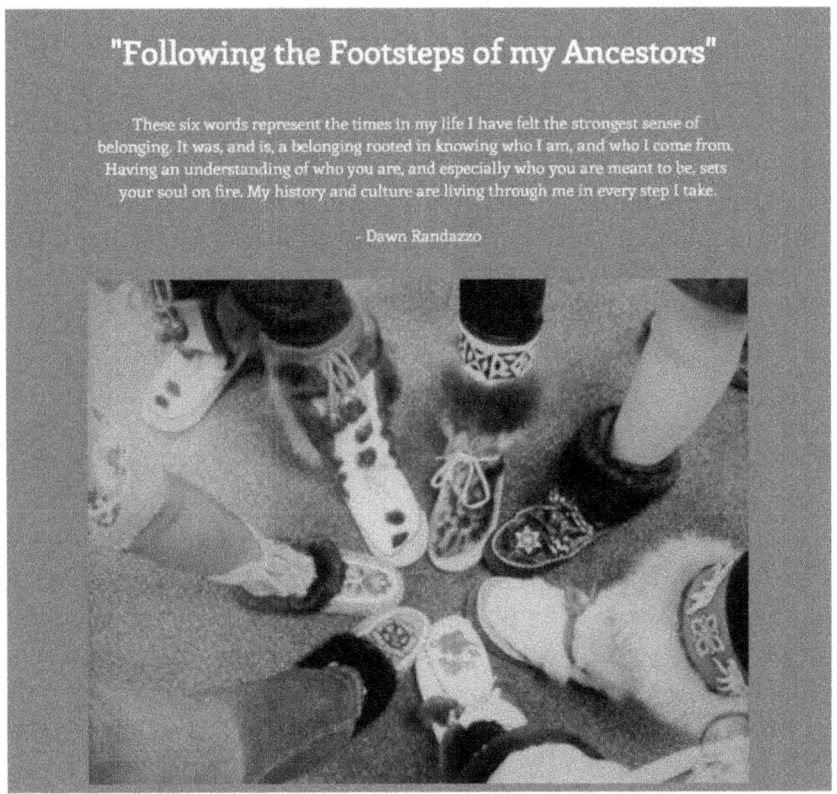

The "power" of this simple portfolio is "unleashed," though, only when it is thoughtfully shared with family, friends, fellow students, and/or as directed by faculty, staff, or advisors. It is through this sharing that we have witnessed students develop deeper and more thoughtful understanding of their individual stories.

An Example from a UAA Class

This past spring (2017) UAA, through its Center for Community Engagement & Learning, offered a course on "Enriching Cultural Identities, Wellness, and Community Education." The course requirements were as follows:

> You will participate in 3 consecutive Friday afternoon 5-hour classes in a workshop format. These sessions emphasize active participation in experiential learning activities. The course includes and requires daily 30-minute personal homework in compassion meditation. Each student will also be required to create 6-word stories in an ePortfolio to reflect and evaluate their learning and to share in the last meeting with students and invited community members. At the last meeting participants will select a personal 6-word story from their ePortfolio to introduce in a community sharing and celebration.

The completed e-portfolio consisted of three pages (or tabs) with each page housing their six-word story assignment. A sample of the stories can be viewed here (the above image is included in this site) http://bit.ly/2y8pd5d.

Based on class evaluations, students valued and found meaning in the class – success! Our e-portfolio service provider, Digication, that works with schools as diverse as Stanford University and LaGuardia Community College frequently showcase this work on a national stage—a nice endorsement for UAA portfolio efforts.

Final Thoughts

As a high impact practice, e-portfolios have been determined to be a valued academic and student affairs tool. The customized use of e-portfolios through six-word stories promotes a sense of belonging, an emotional quality that research shows is valuable in producing stronger academic performance.6 Our experience also shows us the e-portfolio can build community and belonging with marginalized constituents.

Thoughtfully deploying a portfolio can be viewed as a major challenge or "headache" since education leaders often view creating a portfolio as too complicated, containing numbers of different and varied artifacts, reflections, and multiple pages--showcase and capstone portfolios come to mind. A simple six-word story portfolio with an image(s) and a short reflection can be a powerful and meaningful instructional strategy. This strategy should be easy to include in a variety of educational contexts. A six-word "wrap" to the article...

Thanks for listening to my story!

Footnotes

1. Roncero-Menendez, S. (2014, May 16). *In Six Words, These Writers Tell You An Entire Story.* Retrieved October 23, 2017, from https://www.huffingtonpost.com/2014/05/16/six-word-story_n_5332833.html
2. *Welcome to The Race Card Project! Send your six words on race.* (n.d.). Retrieved October 23, 2017, from http://theracecardproject.com/
3. Watson, C., Kuh, G. D., Rhodes, T., Light, T. P., & Chen, H. L. (2016). EPortfolios – The Eleventh High Impact Practice. *International Journal of ePortfolio, 6*(2), 65-69. Retrieved October 23, 2017, from www.theijep.com.
4. Schaffhauser07/09/14, D. (2014, July 09). *Why Large-Scale E-Portfolios Make Sense.* Retrieved October 24, 2017, from https://campustechnology.com/articles/2014/07/09/why-large-scale-e-portfolios-make-sense.aspx
5. McCoy, K (2016, July 28). *Exploring cultural identity through digital storytelling.* Retrieved October 24, 2017, from http://greenandgold.uaa.alaska.edu/blog/44379/campus-community-exploring-cultural-identity-resurrection-digital-storytelling/
6. Walton, Gregory M, Cohen, Goeffrey L., Cwir, David, & Spencer, Steven, J. (2012) Mere Belonging: The Power of Social Connectedness. *Journal of Personality and Social Pscyhology, 102*(3), 513-532.

References

McCoy, K. (2016, July 28). *Exploring cultural identity through digital storytelling.* Retrieved October 24, 2017, from http://greenandgold.uaa.alaska.edu/blog/44379/campus-community-exploring-cultural-identity-resurrection-digital-storytelling/

Norris, M. (n.d.). *Welcome to The Race Card Project! Send your six words on race.* (n.d.). Retrieved October 23, 2017, from http://theracecardproject.com/

Roncero-Menendez, S. (2014, May 16). *In Six Words, These Writers Tell You An Entire Story.* Retrieved October 23, 2017, from https://www.huffingtonpost.com/2014/05/16/six-word-story_n_5332833.html

Schaffhauser07/09/14, D. (2014, July 09). *Why Large-Scale E-Portfolios Make Sense.* Retrieved October 24, 2017, from https://campustechnology.com/articles/2014/07/09/why-large-scale-e-portfolios-make-sense.aspx

Walton, G., Cohen, G., L., Cwir, D., and Spencer, S. (2012) Mere Belonging: The Power of Social Connectedness. *Journal of Personality and Social Pscyhology, 102*(3), 513-532.

Watson, C., Kuh, G. D., Rhodes, T., Light, T. P., & Chen, H. L. (2016). EPortfolios – The Eleventh High Impact Practice. *International Journal of ePortfolio, 6*(2), 65-69. Retrieved October 23, 2017, from www.theijep.com.

Paul Wasko, University of Alaska Anchorage
Tommy Lee Woon, Naropa University

E-Portfolio as a Multidimensional Learning Experience for Preservice Teachers

With the increased use of technology in teaching and learning, preservice teachers nationwide are required to attend courses to help them integrate technology tools in their future classrooms. This situation is not different in the college of education at my university. During a technology integration course, students were directed, not only to create and evaluate these tools, but also to compile their artifacts in an e-portfolio to be presented to teachers and future employers as part of a demonstration of learning. Many researchers argue that some of the advantages of creating e-portfolios over paper-and-pencil portfolios, especially in a technology integration course, are the ability to include multimedia and the ease of sharing with others. Furthermore, portfolios can provide a richer, deeper, and more accurate assessment of what students have learned compared to traditional methods that only measure what students know at a specific point in time.

The course in the current practice was offered 3-hours weekly for 16 weeks face-to-face and online. The course was to help students become familiar with classroom technology applications and integration for teaching and classroom management. The e-portfolio was used as a learning and assessment tool by 350 undergraduates and graduate preservice teachers from ages 18 – 40 years. The teaching method was non-lecture and project-based activities. Learning materials were short videos, screencasts, and online reading. Although most of the projects were similar for graduate and undergraduate students, the focus and the final products were unique for each student based on major, content area, and graduate level. Students worked through projects with the guidance of their instructor and the support of their peers individually and were free to post online questions for help or clarification. During the weekly activities, the instructor introduced the topic and the students worked on the projects supported by the learning materials. Most of the activity time was dedicated to hands-on projects. The final project was creating a personal e-portfolio to compile and present all projects created during the semester.

Students developed technology projects, such as Smart Board lessons, digital video, and animation for teaching and learning, WebQuest, selecting and utilizing technology for students with exceptionalities, digital whiteboard, online collaboration tools, utilizing social network for teaching, and finding and using games for teaching and learning. Students' projects were evaluated weekly and received feedback on their progress. For example, I assigned the topic, "Distance teaching and learning and the role of the Internet." As a project for this topic, students were asked to develop a WebQuest, including deciding the lesson based on their content area, developing the lesson instruction, collecting lesson information, web links, images, videos, assessment, and, finally, creating and designing the WebQuest. At the end of the semester, students compiled all project artifacts in an individualized e-portfolio using Google Sites or Wix. Finally, students developed and then presented their e-portfolio to classmates.

The method of creating learning projects and e-portfolios in current practice resulted in several positive outcomes echoed in students' feedback and course grades. Many students favored this type of learning environment, where it gave them a sense of control to create personalized projects, manage and support their learning goals, and communicate their questions and progress with others. Social learning theorists (i.e., Bandura, 1970; Vygotsky, 1978) suggest that the learning process is complex, multidimensional, and connected to the learner's experiences, and, therefore, they emphasize the importance of the learner's social context. The use of e-portfolio allowed students to ask, communicate and observe their peers' work and ideas to construct their own projects. The majority of students emphasized the importance of connecting the projects to their own context and experience. For example, a student said, "the instructor allowed us to work on the assignments in the way that we thought would work best for us and he was always here to help whenever I needed." Other students preferred to work at their own pace and be creative, or, as one student put it, "The learning setting allowed me to explore my creative side because we were given the freedom to work on our projects on our own pace and I had plenty of time to complete all work."

Finally, utilizing the e-portfolio as an assessment tool helped improve preservice teachers' perceived self-efficacy and intention to use technology in their future classrooms. This improvement was evident from the comparison of the survey results of students' self-efficacy and intention given to them at the first and the last weeks of the semester. According to the theory of planned behavior (Ajzen, 1985, 1991), individuals' behavior can be changed by modifying their intention to act on this behavior by involving both affective and cognitive processes that lead to positive changes. Further, individuals will intend to take an action (incorporate technology tools in their future classrooms) when they are confident in their ability to do so. In the current practice, students showed positive changes in their self-efficacy and intention in both graduate and undergraduate sections through their course comments and surveys results. Many students indicated that creating the e-portfolio helped them to share their work with others and integrate the produced projects in their own classrooms. A student said, "I was able to take a lot of the things I learned about and created and pass it along to my co-teachers. The e-portfolio gave me a desire and ability to learn more about technology and how to use it in my own classrooms." Another student indicated that connection between the e-portfolio projects and seeing its benefits for job seeking and in class teaching improved her self-efficacy by saying, "There was such an array of technology options presented in this class. It showed me that finding material to use in my future classrooms is easier than I thought. It opened my eyes to new and helpful technologies that can be useful in the classroom and very beneficial for my teachings, no matter which subject it is. My e-portfolio is something I will use definitely in my future on my resume."

In conclusion, the use of e-portfolio as learning and assessment tools with preservice teachers improved their self-efficacy and academic achievement, and has the potential to change their intention to use technology in their future classroom.

Mohamed Ibrahim, Arkansas Tech University

ePortfolios Help Students Integrate Their Learning

Introduction

Transitioning to college can be a difficult experience for students at our two-year, open-access institution. Many students are from underserved populations such as first-generation, racial minorities, and economically challenging homes. Finly and Mc-Nair (2013) found such students are even more likely to benefit from the implementation of High Impact Practices (HIPs). Two important High Impact Practices (HIP) were brought together in the development of a first-year experience (FYE) course for biology and chemistry majors. The FYE course is a HIP that prepares students for the types of professions available to biology and chemistry majors. ePortfolios were added as a way to help students integrate their learning across the different course modules. ePortfolios are the main portal into the FYE course.

FYE Design and Structure

Instructors from the biology and chemistry departments identified student-learning outcomes and selected the elements that should be included in the first-year experience course: transitioning to college, developing a career plan, and beginning to establishing their professional identity.

Initially, the course focused on study skills, and students did not seem engaged in the course content. Most FYE students did not appreciate or relate to course topics that anticipated potential challenges they might face in their college education. The weekly topics were only loosely connected under a broad umbrella of becoming educated for a scientific career in a vague future.

In an effort to engage students and help them integrate their learning, the chemistry and biology departments began a course redesign process that involved the incorporation of a common read and the development of a learning eportfolio to compile students' FYE experiences.

ePortfolio Design and Structure

Faculty looking for a way to make learning visible to both students and faculty chose to use eportfolios. The FYE course was organized into pre-class assignments, in-class work, and post-class assignments. This work was documented in the eportfolio. As part of their pre-class work, students brought in information related to the class topic. For instance, students were asked to bring a copy of their degree audits. During class, students analyzed how this information fit into different aspects of their career and were coached on constructing a good quality artifact such as an effective career plan. The goal of each post-class assignment was to upload a peer-reviewed artifact related to the week's course topic. After posting their artifact, students were asked to reflect on its relevance for their learning and future goals. The eportfolio was thus used to collect, organize, and display these artifacts.

Students were asked to use their eportfolios each week to build upon their previous work to deepen and extend their understanding of what the expectations are for a person in their desired career. The eportfolio became a repository of their learning activities that they could use to consult and reflect upon. At the end of the course, students were invited to reflect upon the work they had compiled in the eportfolio to examine what they learned about their future profession and the path needed to achieve it. The eportfolio helped students see the multifaceted nature of their career path, which was an evolutionary step for students transitioning from high school to college.

The success of eportfolios in this FYE course depends on six high impact practices: high performance expectations, significant investment of time and effort, feedback, reflection and integration, and public demonstration of competence. High performance expectations were established through clear directions each week in how to set up the portfolio and what artifacts to include. Each week students worked on their eportfolio as part of the course activities, which required a significant investment of time and effort. Students received weekly feedback on their eportfolios through grades that were available before the next class session. Students engaged in weekly and a cumulative reflection. The weekly reflections asked students to connect the class activity to other activities outside the class. For instance, when the class focused on note-taking skills, students were asked to identify situations in which effective note taking would be beneficial in their career. At the end of the term, students were asked to write a longer final course reflection that asked them to examine the course as a whole. Finally, students used the eportfolio as a means of public display of their learning through in-class presentations.

Lessons Learned

Faculty need training. Kuh & O'Donnel (2013) raise the question of what faculty/staff expertise is needed to develop a High Impact Practice. In the case of chemistry and biology faculty integrating eportfolios, they needed technological and pedagogical support as they began. Most faculty were unfamiliar with the platforms available for eportfolios, so the consultants recommended an open source platform that would be fairly easy for faculty and students to learn. Since the college does not have instructional technology support, the consultants were English professors who have researched eportfolios and used eportfolios in their courses.

Students need training and support. Students needed clear, simple instructions to set up their portfolio sites. If the eportfolio is to be taken seriously, it must be integrated seamlessly into the course such that the course would be incomplete without it. Each week students must use the eportfolio to archive their learning and to reflect upon what it means for their development.

Implications for Implementation

Eynon & Gambino (2017, p. 195) argue that "Integrated into the FYE, ePortfolio practice helps new students identify strengths and growth areas and develop an academic plan." To realize the promise of eportfolios, administrators and faculty need to engage in sufficient planning. They need to identify the technology that will be used for the eportfolio and establish how support for the technology will be made available for faculty and students. Faculty also need to establish how the eportfolio will be used each week to support student learning.

In addition to careful planning, faculty and administrators should establish how the eportfolio's effectiveness will be evaluated. How will faculty and students know that the eportfolio is truly achieving its promise of helping students to "identify their strengths and growth areas"?

References

Eynon, B. & Gambino, L. M. (2017). *High mpact ePortfolio practice.* VA: Stylus.

Finly, A. & McNair, T. (2013). *Assessing underserved students' engagement in high-impact practices.* Retrieved from https://www.aacu.org/sites/default/files/files/assessinghips/AssessingHIPS_TGGrantReport.pdf

Kuh, & O'Donnell. (2013). *Ensuring quality & taking high-impact practices to scale.* Washington, D.C.: Association of American Colleges and Universities.

Brenda Refaei, University of Cincinnati Blue Ash College
Alan Lundstedt, University of Cincinnati Blue Ash College

Afterword

In conjunction with compiling this collection, we were engaged in further research of our own on HIPs. One aspect that struck us was the relative scarcity of studies on the effect of HIPs on student learning. In a report prepared for the Association of American Colleges and Universities (AACU), Swaner and Brownell (2008) lament that while existing scholarship supports the positive impact of such practices, "the strength of evidence for these outcomes' power is weakened by the limitations of existing research" (p. 2).

Our hope is that, spurred by the tips showcased in this collection, many of our readers will not only employ some of the strategies in their classrooms, but will also take the next steps by investigating the outcomes of such approaches on student learning and engaging in the scholarship of teaching and learning (SoTL) through publication of their findings.

Reference

Swaner, L., & Brownell, J. (2008). Outcomes of high impact practices for underserved students: A review of the literature. Washington, DC: AACU.

About the Authors

Charlie Sweet, Ph.D. (Florida State University, 1970), is the Co-Director of the Teaching & Learning Center at Eastern Kentucky University. With Hal, he has collaborated on over 1100 published works, including 19 books, literary criticism, educational research, and novels (as Quinn MacHollister).

Hal Blythe, Ph.D. (Louisville, 1972), is the Co-Director of the Teaching & Learning Center. With Charlie, he has collaborated on over 1100 published works, including 19 books (eight in New Forums' popular It Works For Me series), literary criticism, educational research, and a stint as ghostwriter of the lead novella for the Mike Shayne Mystery Magazine.

Russell Carpenter, Ph.D. (University of Central Florida, 2009), is Executive Director of the Noel Studio for Academic Creativity and Program Director of Applied Creative Thinking at Eastern Kentucky University where he is also Associate Professor of English. Dr. Carpenter has published on the topic of creative thinking, among other areas, including three texts by New Forums Press: *Introduction to Applied Creative Thinking* (with Charlie Sweet and Hal Blythe, 2012), *Teaching Applied Creative Thinking* (with Charlie Sweet, Hal Blythe, and Shawn Apostel, 2013), and *It Works for Me, Flipping the Classroom: Shared Tips for Effective Teaching*, (with Hal Blythe and Charlie Sweet, 2015). He has guest edited or co-edited special issues of the *Journal of Faculty Development* on social media and the future of faculty development. In addition, he has taught courses in creative thinking in EKU's Minor in Applied Creative Thinking, which was featured in the *New York Times* in February 2014, and rhetoric and composition in the Department of English.

www.ingramcontent.com/pod-product-compliance
Lightning Source LLC
Chambersburg PA
CBHW080450170426
43196CB00016B/2751